REGIONAL RESTRUCTURING UNDER ADVANCED
CAPITALISM

CROOM HELM SERIES IN GEOGRAPHY AND
ENVIRONMENT
Edited by Alan Wilson, Nigel Thrift, Michael Bradford and
Edward W. Soja

CONCEPTS AND TECHNIQUES
IN URBAN ANALYSIS
Bola Ayeni

URBAN HOUSING PROVISION
AND THE DEVELOPMENT
PROCESS
David Drakakis-Smith

URBAN TRANSPORT
PLANNING
John Black

HUMANISTIC GEOGRAPHY AND
LITERATURE
Douglas C.D. Pocock

DAVID HARVEY'S GEOGRAPHY
John L. Paterson

PLANNING IN THE SOVIET
UNION
Judith Pallot and Denis J.B. Shaw

CATASTROPHE THEORY AND
BIFURCATION
A.G. Wilson

THEMES IN GEOGRAPHIC
THOUGHT
Milton E. Harvey and
Brian P. Holly

REGIONAL LANDSCAPES AND
HUMANISTIC GEOGRAPHY
Edward Relph

CRIME AND ENVIRONMENT
R.N. Davidson

HUMAN MIGRATION
G.J. Lewis

THE GEOGRAPHY OF
MULTINATIONALS
Edited by Michael Taylor and
Nigel Thrift

URBAN GEOGRAPHY
David Clark

RETAIL AND COMMERCIAL
PLANNING
R.L. Davies

MODELLING HOUSING
MARKET SEARCH
Edited by W.A.V. Clark

INSTITUTIONS AND
GEOGRAPHICAL PATTERNS
Edited by Robin Flowerdew

MATHEMATICAL
PROGRAMMING METHODS FOR
GEOGRAPHERS AND PLANNERS
James Killen

THE LAND PROBLEM IN THE
DEVELOPED ECONOMY
Andrew H. Dawson

THE GEOGRAPHY OF
WESTERN EUROPE
Paul L. Knox

THE GEOGRAPHY OF
UNDERDEVELOPMENT
Dean Forbes

GEOGRAPHY SINCE THE
SECOND WORLD WAR
Edited by R.J. Johnston
and P. Claval

REGIONAL RESTRUCTURING UNDER ADVANCED CAPITALISM

Edited by
PHIL O'KEEFE

CROOM HELM
London & Sydney

© 1984 P. O'Keefe
Croom Helm Ltd, Provident House, Burrell Row,
Beckenham, Kent BR3 1AT
Croom Helm Australia Pty Ltd, First Floor, 139 King Street,
Sydney, NSW 2001, Australia

British Library Cataloguing in Publication Data

Regional restructuring under advanced capitalism.
    1. Regional economics
    I. O'Keefe, Phil
    330.9   HT391

    ISBN 0-7099-1943-3

Printed and bound in Great Britain by
Biddles Ltd, Guildford and King's Lynn

CONTENTS

ACKNOWLEDGEMENTS

The essays in this volume were originally prepared
for a week-long conference held at the Institute
Pedagogique in Walferdange, Luxembourg, in June,
1980. A number of individuals and institutions
contributed greatly to the ability of the Clark
University Regional Development Unit to organise the
meeting.

Professor Gerald J. Karaska of Clark's School
of Geography contributed sage advice and counsel in
locating and obtaining appropriate resources. The
meeting was supported by funds provided by Mr. and
Mrs. Henry J. Leir as part of the Clark-Luxembourg
Conference Series. Dr. Gaston Shaber, the Director
of the Institute Pedagogique, was a gracious host in
Walferdange. The staff of the Institute was unfail-
ingly helpful; we wish especially to acknowledge
Anna who provided the essential ingredients for a
successful 8-day meeting - wholesome and plentiful
food and drink.

The citizens and Mayor of Walferdange welcomed
us warmly and invited us to participate in their
National Day celebration which coincided with our
stay.

To each of the above, the authors and conference participants are grateful for the opportunity
to come together across space and cultures in common
endeavour.

INTRODUCTION

This volume contains some of the papers presented
at the Luxembourg conference on regional development. In the period between the conference and the
publication of this manuscript several publications
have appeared that reflect themes discussed around
the conference table. The papers in this volume,
however, are grouped around a more theoretical
focus, namely what is the current transition that
capital is undergoing and what possibilities exist
for building a socialist initiative in the present
climate?
     The conference was not fortuitous. It reflect-
ed a growing concern and effort to address the in-
adequacies of much socialist analysis of the
'regional problem', an inadequacy that limited
class analysis and intervention. From the United
States participants, there was a strong emphasis on
theory building, an emphasis tinged with the possibilities and problems of structuralism. In
contrast, the European participants, especially the
English, were less enamoured with the prospect of
such theoretical effort. Instead, they emphasised
the importance of considering major political
initiatives that were emerging from the working
class and socialist movements. In short, there were
significant, and genuine, debates and disagreements.
We share some of these debates and disagreements in
the hope that a wider readership can enhance the
quality and the direction of a broader debate.

Levels of Abstraction and Levels of Analysis
This general issue arose in two ways. First, in the
papers, there are presentations that, implicitly or
explicitly, use the notion of level. Clearly, the
notion of level indicates the importance of

1

abstraction but is there a definitive hierarchy of abstraction? The notion of levels of abstraction arises because of the varying degree of detail associated with abstract models. In Volume I of Capital, Marx abstracts from the competitive process of allocating surplus value among capitalists. The focus is entirely on the accumulation of value. In Volume III, this competitive process is introduced at the cost of a uniform notion of value which now bifurcates into separate value and price components. Levels of abstraction and analysis are not simply differences between general and specific, between abstract and concrete: they are generic terms that contain a fundamental dialectic. How can analysis of mode of production be integrated with analysis of social formations? No scheme or hierarchy has yet been established, and accepted, that allows a socialist analysis of regions to be adequately undertaken.

Secondly, almost whatever we define them to mean, the papers in this volume operate at very different levels. Much discussion took place about both the relation of "theoretical work", in whatever forms, and more "concrete" studies and how to relate both efforts to forms of political intervention. Some theory is cast at such a general level of abstraction that it gives only the broadest hint of its application or implication for ongoing political struggle. Some concrete studies are so concrete, so tied to the empirical problems they address that they lose a larger sense of the overall flow of history. Only some form of abstraction can isolate the structural from the conjunctural. Both theorist and caseworker clearly require a "monkey on their back", essentially political practice.

Hypermobility of Capital

Capital mobility is a key focus in socialist analysis of regions. However, is capital mobility a principal strategic option associated with the current crisis by which capital ensures its own expanded reproduction? Is capital mobility now quantitatively more important and fulfilling a qualitatively different function? Some of the US participants argued strongly that the velocity of capital, the rate of changing investment decisions, is a central weapon in capital's strategic arsenal. Using the expression "hypermobility of capital" enables them to capture metaphorically what they

identify as a new lever of exploitation specifically associated with the current capitalist
reorganisation.

Certainly the metaphor has heuristic value
enabling an understanding of the ways in which
capital can make use of the unequal forms of the
organisation of the labour force. Additionally,
insights can be gained into the use that capital
makes of different political frameworks. In particular, attention focused on the issue of federalism
which, as it devolved significant legislative
authority to localities and regions, had become a
major constitutional resource for capital. The
mosaic of local differences allows translocal
decision makers to pick and choose among sites and
situations: the state creates a buyer's market for
capital. If this is true for a subnational level,
then how much more significant transnationally in
such institutions are the European Economic
Community?

Finally, there was discussion about whether or
not there was considerable variability within the
current international practice of capital. Those
who approached the issues from a structural analysis of changes within the capitalist mode of
production argued that variability should not be
exaggerated. Natural resources, for example, cannot
be exploited unless capitalism has the benefit of
liquidity. Others, who essentially approached the
methodological issues from concrete engagement with
historical struggles, argued that too much emphasis
was placed on the uniformity of capital, a uniformity that was not apparent in class struggle in
regions. Underlying these different interpretations
were different strategies for organising and a
significantly different interpretation of the role
of the working class in the transition to socialism.

Deskilling, Female Workers and Sexism

This conglomeration of problems arose in many con-
texts. Although it is uncontestable that capital
has substituted machinery for human labour, what
precisely do we mean by deskilling? Does it apply
both within and between generations of workers?
A tendency to equate deskilled labour with female
workers was noted and opposed. The labelling of
work done by women as less skilled is a product not
only of the nature of work but also the processes
of job definition and the social processes of the
allocation of specific groups of workers to

particular types of jobs. These processes must be investigated, not assumed.

In fact, there are a series of critical problems that socialist analysis of regional change must address. Is the availability of work for women and the female activity rate in regions of crisis still significantly lower than the national average? What is the relationship between unemployment and the reserve army of labour, and how is this relationship affected by the relative increase in female labour? How can the traditional, patriarchal structures of male craft unions be encouraged to support a position, despite the enormous personal dislocation, that new jobs are not inadequate "because they are for women" but because the wages and conditions are appallingly bad? More questions than answers in an area that requires much political engagement.

Politics, Ideology and Economics

Several points emerged around these debates. Firstly, the production process, at local and regional level, cannot be considered simply as an economic activity. Secondly, similar economic activities and conditions produce very different trade union, community and political responses. Most importantly, there is a clear tension between the increasingly global level of economic activity and the localised nature of the working class response.

It is such tensions that we seek to understand. We hope that these essays will further that understanding and inform socialist action.

QUESTIONS OF METHOD IN REGIONAL ANALYSIS

Gustavo Fahrenkrog

QUESTIONS OF METHOD IN REGIONAL ANALYSIS

The question of method cannot be left aside when discussing the nature of regional analysis. Massey (1978) argues that many debates hinge on methodological issues, but that the implications of the debates go way beyond methodology. In fact, what appear to be methodological questions are very often political issues couched in a "scientific" debate. No political position can avoid methodological questions.

Before considering the relation between 'politics' and method in regional analysis, we will concentrate briefly on a question which is central to an understanding of this relation.

What is the Purpose of Socialist Regional Analysis?

Any discourse, whatever its nature, has, at its origin, a pertinent question. This question might have originated in the context of another, much wider discourse. 1. In our case, the question finds its origin and thus its pertinence in the Marxist discourse. It is because of this discourse, that we ask about the purpose of undertaking regional analysis, since Marxist discourse assumes that the meaning, which is created by regional analysis, is the basis of the social practice. There is no social production of meaning void of a specific social practice. Regional analysis is no exception to this.

A Marxist discourse has to distinguish at least two substantially different answers to this question. Both are the result of the social practice of the agents which the discourse distinguishes in capitalist societies.

The Marxist discourse distinguishes, first, a bourgeois and hegemonic discourse, one which assigns to regional analysis the same function which any other production of social meaning has in its context: the reproduction of its conditions of existence as agents in a class society. To be able to do so, it has to have at least the following two characteristics: it has to negate its function in social class practice and simultaneously explain the phenòmena to which it is referring. One way of negating its role in class practice is by declaring itself 'scientific', implying by it a particular and privileged relation to the 'real' which places the discourse above and outside the sphere of struggle, which is labelled 'ideological'. Nevertheless, it has to give a meaning to its social practice, and thus has to be able to explain and forecast, for example, spatial phenomena. One cannot say that bourgeois theories of regional organisation are wrong because they do not explain the 'hidden' class nature of the regional problems. They do not hide class phenomena because, in the discourse on which they are based, there is no place for the concept of class; nor are those theories, by definition wrong since they have to be able to explain and provide instruments for bourgeois social practice. If the discourse was useless in giving meaning to bourgeois class practice (thus wrong), it would not exist as such or would have to be replaced by another bourgeois discourse which fulfils the two requirements outlined above.

The Marxist discourse distinguishes further the discourse corresponding to the workers' class interest and thus its objective social practice. Regional analysis has, in the context of the working class production of meaning for social practice, the function of explaining two, to a certain extent different, problems.

First, it is necessary to study the effects of capital's organisation of space on the working class. It informs the workers' social practice under capitalism. Thus, it is a discourse which has its useful effect in class struggle. In Laclau's (1977) terminology, it is a 'ruptural' discourse, one which intends to break the existing class relations. Hence in a capitalist social formation, regional analysis analysed from the vantage point of the working class has as its function the understanding of problems posed by the spatial organisation of society, with the aim of engaging with that knowledge in political struggle.

For an example of this function, let us take Massey's (1978) discussion of the insight which

regional analysis can give to working class political struggle. Arguing about the question of regional
separatist movements, she says that capitalism
necessarily proceeds by accumulating fixed capital
unevenly in space and that this operates quite
frequently in a divisive manner upon the working
class. It sets workers of one area against workers
of another, instead of concentrating popular dis-
content on the bourgeois character of the phenomena of uneven accumulation. Regional analysis, with
a working class position, should engage in clarifying this point instead of obscuring it as some of
the so-called 'underdevelopment' and 'unequal
development' theories do. But this is not the only
insight which regional analysis can give to the
working class political struggle. The unequal and
anarchic organisation of productive processes in
space under capitalism can be shown to be highly
wasteful of social labour. Capitalists do not only
extract surplus value from the working class in
general but also subject the working class to social
costs which are much higher, through the destruction
of accumulated past labour. The uneven organisation
of productive processes in space in capitalists'
search for profits constantly requires the building
anew of general conditions of production (roads,
railways, ports, etc.), of the individual and
collective conditions for the reproduction of the
labour forces (from schools to housing), and of the
productive units themselves (factories, plants),
long before their useful life as means of (re)-
production or material circulation has been over.
Take for example the closure in the coal mining
areas of Limburg in South Holland in the sixties.
In less than two decades, this area has been subjected to a double reconversion. First the closure
of 'unprofitable' collieries with the consequent
social loss of accumulated past labour. Then the
building of new infrastructure for the industry
which had to be 'attracted' to the area added to the
'reeducation' of the labour force. More recently,
the area has experienced a new exodus of industries
located only a decade ago (e.g. Phillips).
     A further problematic where regional analysis
might contribute to the working class discourse and
social practice in a capitalist society is the understanding of classes in space and the need to confront the capitalist with an organisation able to
react to a changing (expanding or decreasing) mobility of the bourgeoisie (see H. Radice edit, (1975)
and G. Fahrenkrog (1979)). These are only a few of

the problems which the working class discourse can
tackle by means of the regional analysis of the
capitalist organisation of space. The problems themselves are specified in the concrete social practice
of the working class, thus are specific to any period in the development of a social formation. In
other words, the problems and answers are conjunctural.

The second area of problems posed by the production of meaning for a working class social practice lies in the understanding of the organisation in
space under socialism and the transition to that
stage. This angle of class discourse will not be
dealt with in this paper. Suffice it to say that the
discourse is a very different one. In the transition,
when the hegemony of the working class is still not
established, it has to continue having some of the
'rupturalist' characteristics; it has to fight it out
against the remaining classes and class fractions.
But the discourse of the transition also has elements which are characteristic of the socialist society. It is a discourse which has to organise society for its social reproduction. Hence it has to
understand and organise social practice of a class-
less society.

What is the Nature of Progressive Discourses in Regional Analysis?

It is in light of the answer to the question of what
is the purpose of socialist regional analysis that we
must discuss the discourses which call themselves
'popular', 'socialist' or 'marxist' of one type or
another. These discourses - which might be many and
varied - all recognise the existence of classes in a
capitalist society and claim to be taking the position of the oppressed one. But there is no necessary
coincidence between this claim and the content of
the discourse. In other words, not all 'socialist'
discourses take the working class position in class
struggle. Even more, not all discourses which take a
class position in struggle have, at their base, the
same tactical and strategical arguments, i.e. there
is more than one discourse which takes up the working class position. 2.

It does not make much sense to review all discourses which deal with the question of spatial development from an explicitly formulated 'socialist'
position in order to discover whether they effectively take that position and inform the workers'
social practice. For the purpose of this paper, we

will analyse only a few of the most representative types of discourses. To this end we will use Massey's (1978) classification which has a similar aim to ours, namely the analysis of the political implications of the different theories and methods of regional analysis.

She distinguishes two types of theoretically and methodologically different approaches to the question of regional analysis. The first type uses abstract formulations and general laws of historical materialism whose spatial effects are studied. In this category she places: the theories which derive from the necessary tendencies of capital to concentrate in space (Holland 1976), the law of value over space (Lipietz 1977), and the definition of the urban as the place of consumption and the region as the place of production (Castells 1977). One could add to those three, the attempts which try to explain the development of urban agglomerations on the basis of one particular aspect of the reproduction of capitalism, such as Lojkine's (1976) hypothesis that capitalist urbanisation is the result of capitalist production of general conditions of production, or Harvey's (1973) early attempts to explain spatial concentrations based on Marx's rent theory and the spatial circulation of surplus. Massey dismisses most of these theoretical arguments on the basis of their abstraction, arbitrariness and political implications which they might have.

The second group of theories, which Massey identifies, are those which take either dependency theory (Carney, Hudson, Ive and Lewis 1975), unequal exchange theories (Lipietz 1977, Sayer 1977), or imperialism theories (Hechter 1975) as the basis for their analysis of the unequal relations between regions. She quite correctly argues that those theories cannot be transplanted from the level which they are intended to explain (relations between nation states) to the relations between intranational spatial units. (This observation is independent of the critiques to which these theories themselves are subject.) Furthermore, regions cannot be given as predefined object. If one makes comparisons between them and points to the 'unequal' or 'peripheral' nature of the relation, the class condition of the organisation of space under capitalism tends to be hidden.

After commenting on these two theoretical positions, Massey suggests that to be able to undertake regional analysis, one should analyse the process of accumulation and spatially unevenly develop-

ed space without any pre-specified delimitation of
it. From the analysis of accumulation, the concept
of geographical organisation in terms of the spatial
division of labour is produced. The spatial division
of labour refers

> to the way in which economic activity corres-
> ponds to geographical inequality in the con-
> ditions of accumulation - the particular kind
> of use made by capitals of such inequality...
> the term does not therefore refer to the
> division of labour between regions. (1978
> p. 114)

The spatial conditions for accumulation are determined by those factors which affect the rate of
profit and are unevenly distributed.

In another article, (Massey 1979), she visual-
ises this process as a series of 'rounds of new
investments', in which the new form of spatial division of labour is evolved in each round.

> At any given historical moment, a whole number
> of different spatial divisions of labour may
> be being evolved by different branches of
> industry... The geographical distribution of
> economic activity which results from the
> evolution of a new form of division of labour
> will be overlaid on, and combined with, the
> pattern produced by previous periods by the
> different forms of division of labour. This
> combination of successive layers will produce
> effects which themselves vary over space,
> thus giving rise to a new form and spatial
> distribution of inequality in the conditions
> of production, as basis for the next round of
> investment. (Massey 1979, p. 235)

Finally, she argues that, although no regions
can be predefined, one has to have some method of
spatial summation, and that the rationale of any
particular form of spatial summary should relate to
its usefulness in analysis. (Massey 1978, p. 121)

After this brief detour into the theoretical
and methodological questions, which are at the basis
of the discourses which specifically state their
'socialist' orientation, we can restate our problem.
Firstly, there is the problem of discussing the discourses' claim to be taking sides in class struggle
and thus explaining spatial problems which affect
the working class social practice. Secondly, we will

have to look at the inconsistencies of the discourse
itself, trying to distinguish the reasons which
might impede an explanation of class phenomena and
hence working class social practice.

The point that will be made here is that many
of the discourses analysed by Massey fail to clarify
the social practice of the working class. This is
not for want of trying, but because of conceptual
problems of the discourse.

There are, first, those discourses which, concentrating on one particular tendency of the development of capitalism (e.g. concentration of capital)
or a specific mechanism within it (e.g. appropriation of land rent, production of general conditions
of production), make them the sole explanatory
factor of the organisation of space. Apart from the
arbitrariness pointed out by Massey, it should be
stressed that their explanatory value to working
class practice can be highly misleading, when taken
out of the conceptual framework in which those mechanisms or phenomena occur. Taken out of the context,
these discourses can easily be integrated into the
bourgeois discourse. The shadowy area of the 'social
-democratic' discourse is full of examples. For
example, the land rent discussion, without an explanation of the role of the different agents, can be -
despite and because of the many Marx quotations -
a bourgeois discourse. In a different context, the
discussion of the reproduction of the general conditions of production, without reference to the
class nature of its provision, is equal to the
bourgeois discourse over infrastructure. The simil-
arities in the appearance of the discourses should
warn us from the dangers of taking out of context
specific phenomena without referring them to the
class nature of the social processes. Hence it is
not the form of the discourse but its use in the
social practice of the different classes which distinguishes its nature. 3.

The second reason why certain discourses might
not give meaning to the social practice of the working class is misinterpretation, misrepresentation
and/or transformation of the concepts on which the
historico-materialist discourse is based. As a
result it is mostly difficult, if not impossible, to
link the analysis of the spatial problematic to the
questions of class practice without having to make a
series of discursive somersaults. Problems of this
sort in the discourse might be many including:

(a) <u>A misinterpretation of the concepts.</u>
These we find typically in discourses which use
the concept of mode of production as equivalent to
the form in which a society (or part of it) produces. This misinterpretation is not uncommon in the
less sophisticated versions of the underdevelopment
theories, and comes, via these discourses, into
theories which try to explain the unequally distributed 'development' of space by comparing the
different 'regions'. The effect of it is that, since
those discourses compare 'societies' with a particular form of producing, closed entities, it is impossible to distinguish classes as groupings of
agents with the same place in the process of production as within those 'societies'. Marxists who
have tried to overcome those difficulties, without
detecting the misconception on which they are based,
have been referring to classes with ad hoc arguments.
(b) <u>A disconnection of concepts.</u>
Castells (1977) presents us with a typical case
when he argues that the concepts to analyse the
economic level of society are production, consumption, distribution and exchange; precisely those
concepts which Marx in the <u>Critique of Political
Economy</u> dismisses as concepts belonging to political economy - thus a bourgeois discourse - because
they are not able to explain the social relations
which are the basis of the class relations within
society. In other words, Castells takes a set of
concepts which in no way fits into the historico-
materialist discourse and thus is unable to give
meaning to the social practice of the working class.
He senses this problem and thus adds - almost as an
annex and unrelated to the rest of the discourse -
a chapter on urban struggle and working class practice. The problem of such an addition is its subject-
ivist character. It originates in the complete disconnection between the analysis of the social
relations and the places which the agents have in
the process of social production.
(c) <u>A transformation of concepts.</u>
It is not uncommon that concepts of historical-
materialism suffer a transformation. This change can
be very often almost imperceptible and be the result
of the changes which the rest of the argument of a
specific discourse imposes on the meaning of the
concepts. Massey, for example, doesn't escape
completely this transformation of the meaning of
concepts when she refers to the 'spatial division of
labour' or the 'branch of industry' in the following

passage: "At any given historical moment, a whole
number of different divisions of labour may be being
evolved by different branches of industry." (1979,
p. 235) Both concepts suffer in this sentence a
'verdinglichung' which is stressed when she argues
that "previous divisions of labour and the ones
resulting from the actual organization of economic
activities combine in successive layers" (ibid).
When speaking about spatial division of labour, in
the Marxist discourse, we are referring to the socially differentiated agents at any given moment of
the development of a social formation; thus to
a condition of the agents. This condition is the
product of the organisation of productive forces –
men and machinery – under certain relations of
production. A social division of labour cannot
impose itself upon another (as layers) unless the
concept is transformed from a concept denoting a
condition of the agents in the process, into an
object or a thing in itself. Equally, a branch cannot produce a division of labour, whether spatial or
not. The division of labour is the concrete
historico-temporal condition in which labour appears
due to the social organisation of production, which
results from specific social rules. Under capitalism
they appear organised in units of production of a
particular kind. The branch is only the summation of
units of production which have certain common denom-
inators. Hence the division of labour cannot be
produced by a 'branch' unless we have collapsed units
of production into branches. Luckily, Massey has not
persisted with the transformed use of these concepts
and thus her discourse is able to make class analysis. It must be emphasized, however, that the dangers
of such a transformation and 'verdinglichung' of
concepts in the Marxist discourse are very real.

We have seen so far a number of reasons why discourses which call themselves socialist might be
seriously impeded in taking the position of the
working class. It need hardly be added that these
are not the only reasons; others can be found.
Nevertheless, the point has been made about the
relation between the concepts and the content of the
discourse. Let us continue now to the next question.

What are the Elements of a Working Class Discourse
about the Organisation of Space?
A number of points were made about the difficulties
of defining a so-called socialist discourse referring to regional issues. First, it had to have a

reason of existence different from the bourgeois discourse. In answer to the first question, the working class discourse existed to produce meaning about spatial phenomena which might affect the working class social practice and hence orient class struggle. The second point, which was made, was that few discourses which do stress their class position had been successful in dealing with class practice because of the inability of the concepts to allow a class analysis. We will have to ask ourselves now: Which are the concepts which <u>do</u> allow the production of meaning about spatial issues for working class social practice?

Working class practice is a practice which develops in struggle with the dominant classes and is conjunctural, thus historically specific. To be able to develop this struggle the working class, and working class discourse, is confronted with three main issues:

First, the fact that somebody is a worker doesn't necessarily imply his/her consciousness of the position he/she occupies as an agent within a particular and historically determined class society. In other words, the 'knowledge' of the position in the class struggle is not necessarily manifest. The 'function' of working class discourse in general and of socialist regional discourse in particular, is to provide meaning, thus 'knowledge' to allow the agents to recognise themselves as agents in the social processes which rules a capitalist society.

The second issue with which the working class struggle is confronted is that of understanding the bourgeois position: i.e. the bourgeois objective interest as a class agent in reproducing capitalist class relations, including the dominant ideology. In other words, the worker engaged in class struggle must have a discourse which allows him to give meaning to the actions of the bourgeoisie and its circumstantial allies, to be able to make political calculations to guide his own struggle. Spatial analysis is one of the parts of this wider discourse. It illustrates certain aspects of the actions which the bourgeois take.

Both problems are impossible to solve without an adequate set of concepts which allow class analysis.

The third, and in the contemporary political debate hotly discussed question, which the discourse has to answer is: to where does this struggle lead us? Class struggle has to have an aim. But to know

16

where we want to get to, we have to answer the
questions of what is socialist society and who
defines what is the socialist society. The answers
to these questions determine, to a great extent, the
ways in which the struggle has to be developed. A
socialist spatial analysis cannot be void of these
aspects. It has to discuss the issues of workers
organisation for struggle in the light of the
discussion of what is the socialist society and the
particular form in which it is organised. 4.

To be able to speak about how space is organised by the dominant class, we will have to define
first what is a class. This is a controversial issue
and has been treated in a more extended form in
Fahrenkrog (1979). Nevertheless, there is one much
quoted definition by Lenin upon which most Marxists
would agree.

> Classes are large groups of people, differing
> from each other by the place they occupy in a
> historically determined system of social
> production, by their relations (in most places
> fixed and formulated by law) to the means of
> production, by their role in the social
> organisation of labour, and, consequently, by
> the dimensions of the social wealth of which
> they dispose and the mode of organising it.
> Classes are groups of people, one of which can
> appropriate the labour of another owing to the
> different places they occupy in a definite
> system of social economy. ('A Great Beginning',
> Collected Works, vol. 29, p. 421.) 5.

Thus every agent, every human individual, has a
particular identification or condition which is not
determined by him or her but by the place occupied
in the system of production. This condition is said
to be his or her objective condition. It is said to
be objective insofar as it can be perceived through
the meaning produced by the historico-materialist
discourse and thus by the agents who perceive their
position through this discourse. It is, however,
possible that an agent, or a number of them, do not
perceive their position in the system of social
production. Classes thus exist without the people
which form them being necessarily conscious of class.
Thus, an agent might and most likely will, be
acting according to a popular discourse (common
knowledge) which is not necessarily the historico-
materialist one.

Hence the historico-materialist discourse has

to distinguish at least the following moments in the
definition of an agent:
- His objective place in the system of
  production.
- His actual, lived idea of that place.

The first one determines what Marxists call class
interest, i.e. the interest which derives from the
place itself. The second defines class position,
i.e. the position of the agent in struggle when confronted with other agents, and acting according to
how he 'sees' them.

The approach to a socialist regional analysis
which will be suggested here makes these concepts
central to the analysis. In fact, it is our convic-
tion that it is not possible to contribute to the
development of class struggle without analysing the
objective positions of the agents, their position in
struggle and the discourse (popular or not) which
sustains the latter. The fact that we are dealing
with spatial issues does not change our argument. It
only specifies the field of inquiry in such a way
that we might concentrate predominantly on the
objective class interest and class position of the
agents which result from the fact that society does
not develop in a vacuum but in a specific geographical space.

This rather general statement has to be specified for the specific historical conditions to be
analysed. It goes without saying that it is methodologically different to contribute to class
struggle by analysing the effects of the organisation of society in space on the struggle in a
contemporary developed country, a contemporary
underdeveloped country, a developed capitalist
country of the 18th century, or the transitional
process in today's China. 6.

Hence, to be able to understand the methodological problems involved in such an analysis, it will
be necessary to limit ourselves to certain types of
social formations, the dominant capitalist ones, and
to illustrate the analysis by means of the methodology followed in a specific case study: The Netherlands, West Brabant after World War II.

The first problem we are confronted with, when
making a study of a social formation with two
antagonistic classes, is that the definition of the
classes and thus the method of their analysis is
different.

The agents belonging to the dominant class, in
our case the bourgeoisie, have to reproduce not only
themselves as individuals but also the system of

social relations on which their dominant position is
based. If the agents do not do that, their position
as dominant agents disappears. For the dominated
classes, it is different. The worker can reproduce
physically in any system of social relations,
capitalist as much as socialist.

This difference means that the capitalist - as
agent occupying a specific position - has to reproduce his objective interest as a class and as
individual in his daily life. Hence, by analysing
the capitalist class position in struggle we will be
analysing also his class interest. Since this reproduction refers only to the social relations, there
might be many political forms in which the bourgeois
class interest is expressed. It can go from a progressive social democracy to the most reactionary
fascist rule. The important point for the question
of method of class analysis is that by determining
the agent's position in the system of social relations we have the main ingredients for analysing his
position in struggle. An agent presents arguments in
different ways, but always reproduces the conditions
of his/her position.

The agent belonging to the dominated class, the
worker, cannot be analysed this way. To determine the
workers' class position in struggle, no such relation between class interest and class position can
be established. The process by which the worker
engaged in class struggle takes up the issues which
represent his own class interest is an <u>individual</u>
one, i.e. every individual agent has to become conscious of his/her condition of being exploited. The
process of acquiring class consciousness is a
complex one and depends on factors such as the
existence of a strong confrontation between classes,
in a crisis and revolutionary conditions, and from
factors such as the existence of organised and class
conscious workers who could help in the transformation of the experience of struggle into class
consciousness proper. (See Mandel, 1970.)

To be able to understand the class position of
the workers, one can only analyse the position in
struggle. 'Objective' class interest is only a
reference for the identification of the agents.
Class position is thus a changing and unstable
condition which has to be reassessed continuously.
Pre-revolutionary and counter-revolutionary situations alternating with each other in a short time
all over the world will illustrate this argument,
e.g. Portugal over the last few years, Chile before
1973 and today, Germany in the 20s and 39.

We will concentrate in this paper on identifying methods which could allow us to make a class analysis of the bourgeoisie and its specific interests in relation to the organisation of space. Why the bourgeoisie? For no theoretical reason as such. The development of concepts to analyse both class positions is necessary. However, we have chosen to develop the analysis of the bourgeois class interest and position in relation to the organisation of space in this paper because of the very sketchy way it has been done until now and the importance it has in terms of understanding the class enemy, his aims and his internal contradictions. Further, there is a more pragmatic reason for making this rather arbitrary decision. The development of the categories has been done in the context of a specific study which intends to analyse the development of planning, planning instruments and planning theory in West Brabant over a certain period. (Leijten, Fahrenkrog 1978.) It is, in our view, impossible to understand these forms of state intervention without understanding the dominant class interest behind it. Since we do not adhere to the 'conspiracy' nor the 'management committee' theory as the basis for understanding state intervention in the interest of the bourgeoisie, it was necessary to determine the specific class and class fraction interest of the bourgeoisie and to confront it with the actual historical form of state intervention in the organisation of space. Hence it was necessary to develop, in the context of the research, some concepts which would allow us to make a class analysis of the bourgeoisie.

Undoubtedly this will not be enough to enable us to understand the role the state has played in class struggle in this particular case. The working class position has to be analysed and only then might we be able to say something more. It must be emphasised, however, that the political analysis of working class position in struggle has been more frequent in Marxist literature, e.g. 'urban struggle', housing struggle, anti-pollution struggle, struggle for or against urban renewal and so on. The analysis is much more straightforward since, as was argued above, the class position of the dominated class can only be understood from struggle itself. The difficulty arises when the class position is confronted with class interest and when the question of political strategy and tactics of the working class arises. This is especially true when the tactics and the confrontation of the working class clash with what could generally be termed the social democratic discourse and its dominance of the 'common sense'.

What is the Problem of Method in the Definition of the Bourgeois Interest in the Organisation of Space?

Let us make here a short digression for the sake of clarity in the argument which follows. Until now, we have stressed the importance of understanding the position which an individual human subject takes in struggle. We are designating the position by the concept <u>agent</u>, which is the place this individual occupies in the reproduction of social life. This place, it was argued, is not only determined by the material world and the social rules which are dominant in their reproduction, but also by the ideas which he/she has about both. This point is discussed in Leijten in this volume.

This formulation presents us with a problem, a methodological and epistemological one, namely the relation between 'individual human subject' and the concept of agent, and the relation of both concepts with the <u>real</u>.

The historico-materialist discourse is full of attempts to establish a relation between the real, the observed reality and the concepts of the discourse. They range from attempts to establish the relation between profits and value categories to the epistemological argument of Marxism being a science which uncovers the real. All of them presuppose the existence of a direct relation between the real and the historico-materialist discourse. The position which will be taken here, and has been discussed elsewhere (Fahrenkrog 1979), is that this direct relation cannot be established, that there is no privileged relation between the discourse and the real, and that the 'validity' of the discourse and its categories can only be established in practice. In the case of the historico-materialist discourse the 'validity' is established in the practice of changing the social relations.

This discussion has several consequences for our argument. First, we will have to distinguish between the entity 'real individual human subject' on the one hand, and the 'observed individual human subject' and the 'agent' - both categories of the historico-materialist discourse - on the other. The latter two have a mutually determining relation <u>within</u> the discourse. Agents are the representation of certain qualities of the observed reality: the individual human subjects; and the observation of human subjects is affected by the fact that Marxism argues that they all have particular places in the reproduction of society.

Secondly, when dealing with 'cases' we will be dealing with observed reality as defined in the discourse, and not with reality itself.

Thirdly, and possibly most importantly for what follows, is the fact that the precision of the categories has to be made within discourse. It is the precision of the relation between observed reality, as for example expressed through observed human subjects, and the rest of the categories of the historical materialist discourse. The aim of it is to increase the usefulness of the discourse for the social practice of some of the observed and interpolated human subjects: the workers.

A further question might be raised at this stage. It is that of the appropriateness of concepts. Why have we chosen to deal with agents and their positions, in the conjuncture, to be able to understand and contribute to class struggle? The answer has been partially given in the preceding arguments. Historical-materialism is a discourse the aim of which is to intervene in the transformation of social life. Therefore, it explains history and contemporary social conditions on the basis of the relations which human beings (as observed) establish between each other. The aim of this explanation is to allow, as already said, the political calculation of the observed human subjects which it interpolates. Although human beings are the object of the discourse and the ones who act and transform the social relations, the discourse has a number of other concepts to explain the nature of the relation between the human beings. A list of examples would include: relations of production, mode of production, social formation, class, class fraction, the economy (with the corresponding 'laws' of value, and the falling rate of profits), ideology (hegemony, consensus, religion), the state, and so on. All these concepts are necessary and operate at different levels of the discourse. They are neither more 'abstract' nor more 'concrete'. They fulfil different functions in the discourse and we shall use them in their particular capacity.

With this brief digression into epistemological and conceptual problems, let us now return to the issues at hand. The aim of the following pages is to understand why a certain category of agents, the bourgeois, act as they do.

Marx distinguished classes on the basis of the position of the agents in the process of production. But how do we distinguish that position? Bettelheim (1976) defines two characteristics which distinguish a bourgeois agent: the ownership and/or possession which he has of the means of production. Ownership is the power to appropriate and dispose of the product obtained whereas possession is the ability to put the means of production to work. The bourgeois has the ownership and possession of the means of production, the worker has none.

This definition, although correct, still does not take us much further than class analysis. Thus, we shall have to specify the concepts of the discourse further.

The notions which traditionally have been used to differentiate the position of different bourgeois agents have been along the line of branches of production (e.g. industrial capital and its subdivisions, capital engaged in agriculture, etc.) or according to the different places the capitalist has in the process of circulation of capital (e.g. merchant capital, productive capital, banking capital, etc.). It is not possible to distinguish other differences except the descriptive ones such as big, medium and small capital; differences which are highly subjective.

It must be emphasized, however, that Marx distinguished another way of differentiating capitals: the different forms of organisation of capital. They could be present in any branch of production or place in the process of circulation. He describes at least three such forms: the individual capital, the stockholding capital (the social capital of directly associated individuals), and the co-operative factories of labourers. Marx does not deal with them in extenso. He only discusses the role which stockholding capital had in overcoming some of the limitations to capital accumulation.

The question now is, what is the distinguishing feature of those forms of organisation of capital? We have argued elsewhere (Fahrenkrog 1979) that this is the different form in which the ownership and possession of the means of production is distributed between the agents. The different forms of organisation of capital resulting from different forms of allocation of ownership and possession between the agents results, when operating in different branches of production, in a specific form of enterprise which is unlike other types of enterprises resulting from other forms of capital organisation in the same branch. It need hardly be added that such differences originate different fractions of capital and class fraction objective interests which are also specific to the question of the organisation of space.

To illustrate this point let us take the two main forms of capital mentioned by Marx: stockholding capital and individual capital. In the last one, the possession of the means of production (the ability to organise the process of production) is clearly in the hands of the owners of that capital. Stockholding capital, because it is social capital of directly associated individuals, has to separate the ownership (which remains in the hand of the stockholder) from the possession of the means of production, transferring the latter into the hands of a manager, chief executive officers and/or managing boards. Apart from the obvious advantages which Marx saw in this form of organisation of capital, notably the increase in the scale of accumulation, it has the additional advantage over individual capital because it can organise - because of the delegation of possession - different units of production and parts of those units in different places. It is thus able to exploit the relative advantages of location, e.g. management in the centres of financial transactions, and labour intensive processes in 'low wage' countries or regions. The mobility of capital increases since it is less bound to the spatial constraints imposed by fixed capital.

In the course of the research, we distinguished a number of different forms of property and possession. They are, as with any list of this sort, historically specific. Still it is interesting to describe these forms since they illustrate a number of relatively common combinations of property and possession under capitalism. Furthermore, it is necessary to point to the practical problems which arise from the legal recognition of the agents and associations and the forms of organisation of capital which are their foundation. We will discuss very briefly, and as example, this combination for Dutch legal associations.

Dutch Legal and Customary Recognition of Agents and Forms of Relations

A number of sources establish the relation between the agents and the form of organisation of capital in the Netherlands. There is first Dutch general law which recognises agents as <u>individuals</u> able to engage in economic relations. The type of economic relation in which the agent might engage are detailed in several legal bodies: the property law, the law regulating contracts, the laws which regulate the exchanges and the company law. The last one establishes the type of relations which the agents can have between themselves and thus determine the framework for the forms of organisation of capital.

Dutch company law (Ondernemingsrecht) distinguishes several forms of relations between agents. Some of them define independent and non-human entities. The relation which human agents can establish without creating a new independent economic agent are three:
- de maatschap - the partnership.
- de vennootschap onder firma, v.o.f. - the firm.
- de commanditaire vennootschap - the "commanditair" partnership.

The differences between them are the extent to which the individuals who associate are personally liable for the activities of the association. The "maatschap" determines full personal liability, the v.o.f. a partial one, and the c.v. two types of personal liabilities: a full one and none.

The associations of agents which create a new, non-human legal entity are for the purpose of organising a capitalist enterprise three: The "Naamloze Vennootschap" (NV), the "Besloten Vennootschap" (BV), and the co-operative. Both NV and BV are partnerships with a social capital distributed in shares and a limited liability. The main difference between them is on the issue of share transfers: the BV has a number of limitations on their transference. The co-operative is an association of independently operating economic agents established for the purpose of providing certain material needs which the individual associates are unable to provide by themselves. With this brief enumeration of the customary and legal recognition of the agents, we can analyse the probable forms of organisation of capital and the legal structure in which they might appear.

(a) <u>Individual capital</u>.

As already argued, ownership and possession of the means of production is in the hands of one individual. There are many variants and different legal forms under which they appear including individual capital (ondernemingsvorm eenmanszaak) and family capital. Family capital has to be

considered as a form of individual capital because
of the direct interdependence of the agents in the
distribution and use of the surplus value.
(b) <u>Simple association of capitals.</u>
This form implies the fusion of two or more
independent capitalists in one unit of an appropriation of surplus value (i.e. one capital). A pre-
condition for its formation is the possibility of
delegating the functions of possession either on one
of the partners or a hired agent. This form might
appear under any legal association established by
Dutch law. The differences between forms and the
possible advantages of using a particular one of
them were considered in our research. We also
analysed the organs established by legal recognition
and the places where the ownership and the possession of the means of production were exercised.
(c) <u>Stockholding capital.</u>
This implies the complete separation of ownership from possession of the means of production. It
is the result of the need of capital to concentrate
at levels which the individual is unable to achieve.
Three forms of stockholding can be distinguished
according to the degree of delegation of possession.

(c1) The unit of production, the unit of appropri-
     ation of surplus value, and the unit of organ-
     isation of capital for production, are one and
     the same. For example, an enterprise consisting
     of one factory owned through shares.
(c2) The unit of extraction of surplus value and the
     unit of organisation of capital for production
     are the same; the production units can be one
     or more and are separated. For example, a
     corporation which owns several productive
     units.
(c3) All three are different. For example, a trust
     owning one or more corporations like the one
     described in (c2).

All three forms of organisation of capital
delegate possession of the means of production at
different levels. The type of delegation determines
the convenience of using one legal form or another.
Both issues were discussed in more detail in our
research.
(d) <u>Co-operatives of capitalists.</u>
A number of independent capitalist producers
set up a separate capital and unit of extraction of
surplus value to produce a good or service necessary
for the realisation of their own product. This unit

operates on a similar basis to a stockholding but is confronted with an insoluable problem in the distribution of the surplus: is it to be through the co-operative or through the enterprise of the members? This makes the profitability and competitiveness of the enterprise very difficult. The limitations and transitional character of such forms have been extensively discussed in the co-operative movements of the Netherlands.

(e) <u>Co-operatives of direct producers</u>.
This form cannot be considered a unit of extraction of surplus value proper, since the direct producer has the ownership of the means of production. Its transitional character and difficulties of surviving are similar to the ones mentioned above.

(f) <u>State enterprises</u>.
Cannot be defined as capital in the usual sense either. They are characterised by the fact that ownership of the means of production is vested in the state. It is thus placed in the insoluable conflict between the general interest of the hegemonic block and its survival as an enterprise in the capitalist system.

These are some of the basic forms of organisation of capital distinguished in our study. Since the legal recognition of them differed widely, several problems arose as to their identification in the research.

<u>What is the Nature of the Bourgeois Class Interest</u>?
With this more extended description of what is meant by forms of organisation of capital, we can return now to our discussion of the bourgeois class interest. It should be noted that, by defining the forms of organisation of capital and the position of the agents in relation to ownership and possession of the means of production, we are clarifying their class identity.

As argued before, capital operates in a branch, or more specifically, in producing a commodity or a useful effect for either capitalist or worker. That unit of capital might have any of the forms of organisation discussed above. Thus we have a combination of both, which can be expressed in the following matrix:

	Form of organistion of capital				
	f1	f2	f3	.....	fn
b1					
b2					
branch or line of production b3					
.					
.					
.					
bm					

Theoretically, all the combinations are possible; but because they are all historically specific the combinations are usually much reduced. Some branches of production have only one or two forms of organisation of capital. For example, in the study of West Brabant, bulk chemicals are only produced by stockholding type c2 or c3. On the other hand, we found, in plastic production, simple associations of capital engaged in producing consumer goods, and stockholding in the production of raw materials. Other branches, such as the building material industry have no stockholds operating in them. Co-operative forms of organisation of capital were identified only in agriculture. These examples indicate that certain commodities are only produced by some forms of organisation of capital, because either the volume of capital necessary is large or because of the low profitability in production.

It need hardly be added that this is not a static phenomenon, but changes continuously in time. At one point, a certain branch of production might have attracted the largest volume and most complex forms of organisation of capital. Today it might only be taken up by individual capitals, co-operatives or the state, e.g. foundries in the 19th century and today. What bourgeois analysts call the 'maturity of a line of production' is certainly important in determining the combination of branch or line of production and forms of capital which operate in it.

Until now we have been referring to combinations of 'branches' of production and forms of organisation of capital. These arguments could be misleading if left without explanation. It was argued above that a branch is a concept which expresses only the summation of units of production with similar production. Thus, a particular unit of production cannot be defined as the combination of a 'branch' with a form of organisation of capital. To be precise, we have to say that it is a production of a certain commodity which is done by a certain form of organisation of capital. For example, it is the production of cast iron motor blocks which is done by individual capital or any other form of organisation of capital. Several of the units of production engaged in producing a certain product and belonging to the same or different forms of organisation of capital constitute a product group. Several product groups constitute in turn a branch.

This precision has a practical repercussion on the question of method of analysis. To be able to understand the objective position of the capitalist agent in the system of social production we have to refer to specific <u>units</u> of production.

Hence we have to deal with 'cases' as observed reality. Conceptually we are not dealing with 'agents' as definitions of positions, but with observed individual human subjects within certain observed and historically specific units of production. The subjects have to be representative of the positions and serve as exemplifications.

The matrix outlined above is not a further disaggregation of a typical study of economic activity according to forms of organisation of capital. It is a matrix of possible case studies organised according to different forms of organisation of capital, producing commodity case studies which hopefully will be representative of a number of similar enterprises. The aim is to determine the class interest of the agents and the common interests between different fractions of the dominant class.

Towards a Socialist Regional Analysis

Until now, we have been speaking about class interest of the agents in general. But a socialist <u>regional</u> analysis specifies the problematic of class struggle to the study of the effects which natural and man-made space has on that struggle. In our view it has to be considered only as an emphasis in the

analysis and has always to be referred to the
general question of class struggle. Space intervenes
in class struggle insofar as its use produces relative advantages for the different agents. Since we
have concentrated, in this paper, on the analysis of
the class interest and class position of the dominant classes, we will review the spatial issues only
insofar as they concern them. As to the working
class, we maintain the argument given above. The
class position of the workers is determined in the
conjuncture and in struggle. It might or might not
coincide with their own class interest. To be able
to make political calculations from the point of
view of the working class, one has to know the class
position in struggle of both classes. The analysis
of the latter has not been made here, but is necessary for any calculation.

Capitalism, like any other mode of production,
organises the production process in such a way that
it is able to produce, appropriate and distribute
the surplus labour. Under capitalism, the mechanism
works through commodity exchange and the creation of
surplus value in the process of production. Hence,
the organisation of production and productive
processes in space is determined by the capacity to
generate surplus value.

The aim of any capitalist, whatever branch of
production he/she is engaged in, is to increase the
appropriation of profits. Several ways of doing so
are available to the individual capitalist. Each one
of these has a distinctive effect on the organisation of productive processes in space.

For production to take place, the capitalist
has to bring together labour, the object of labour,
and the material productive forces. The most simple
form of increasing the productivity of labour is the
concentration at the same place of a certain number
of labourers doing the same work. Even this simple
form of co-operation of labour implies a decision by
the capitalist agent to locate the process in space.
He/she has to provide a roof, pool together the
implements of labour, stock raw materials and so on.
This means that before initiating any production at
all, the capitalist has to make a decision about
location which takes into consideration sources of
raw materials, location of consumers, means of
transport, possibilities of expanding production at
the place in question, and possible variations in
all those and other factors that may intervene. The
outcome of such a decision must enable him or her to
produce commodities at their current market price or

below. With every change in price of the commodity, the capitalist will have to reconsider the new conditions of production. In certain cases, he/she will be able to adapt to those changes without changing location. But, as soon as the production costs of the commodity he/she is producing are higher than the current market price, he/she will have either to stop production completely or reorganise the production process under the new conditions and that might involve a relocation.

Furthermore, this is a process in which the search for profits of all capitalists organises production and the reproduction of society unequally in space. Each round of investment responds to the unequal conditions created by the former. Capital uses these 'inequalities' in order to maximise profits. In time, these relative advantages might disappear, thus making the fixed capital investment redundant much before the useful life of machinery and equipment, the general conditions of production and the housing and installations for collective consumption and reproduction of the labour force has ended.

Capital has thus to move in search of new relative advantages, and, once they are found, to produce anew all the general conditions of production and the installations necessary for the reproduction of labour at high costs for society at large and with an enormous waste of social labour.

In this process of location and relocation, in their struggle to keep the relative advantages frozen in time and/or in getting new general conditions of production allocated, the capitalist agent has or might have common interests with other capitalists thus constituting alliances of class fractions. These class fraction alliances will vary over time in relation to the variations of the capitalist's class interest.

For example, Philips (ELA), as representative of a particular fraction of capital, located a plant for the production of professional audio and vision equipment in Breda in 1962, after a detailed study of the labour conditions which indicated high levels of unemployment and predominantly non-unionised labour in the region. At about the same time, a number of other industries, representing other fractions, located for the same reasons. At the end of the seventies, these 'inequalities' and advantages had disappeared. For some of these fractions, it has meant having to get Belgian workers to commute at high costs to the enterprise. For Philips,

this has not been a problem since they tapped a part
of the labour reserves which has neither diminished
nor become organised, i.e. female labour. Philips
does not, therefore, participate in the industrial-
ists' lobby to work against this particular
'problem', namely the disappearance of the inequalities and the relative advantages.

The number of specific fractional interests
generated in this way are many. They have to do with
historically specific questions such as:
- labour and its cost of reproduction,
  qualifications, organisation, transport,
  housing.
- raw material costs, origin, transport and
  changes in those factors.
- general conditions of production, their
  individual cost, location and provision.
- the location of markets and the variation
  in them.

The formulation of the problems varies according to the product group and the form of organisation of capital. The combination of alliances of
fractional interests which might arise are conjunctural. For example, the fraction of stockholding,
type c3, in one line of production might have a
common objective interest in one of the factors
enumerated above with the fraction of individual
capitals in a completely different line of production.

Finally, the reason for trying to understand
the fractional interest arising from the objective
conditions of the unit of production in its search
for profits, is the possibility it gives for making
calculations as to its possible development. Here,
we return to our point of departure. This calculation is one of the points which form part of a
political calculation of the working class, in that
it defines the objective limits in which the
capitalist can operate. It further allows an understanding of the role of the state in the managing of
the organisation of space under capitalism and the
objective interests which it benefits. Thus the
discussion of regional analysis is placed in the
context of working class struggle, and serves as a
base for the definition of its strategy and tactics.

Conclusion
This paper has been an attempt to point to some of
the methodological issues which a working class
analysis of the 'regional problem' should consider.

As such, it is incomplete and sketchy, and intended
mainly as an instrument of discussion. It should not
be considered as a recipe for a Marxist analysis of
spatial problems for several reasons. It is a
discourse which has at its base the taking of a
position within the historico-materialist discourse.
There may be other interpretations of the historico-
materialist discourse, the social democratic being
one of them. It is not a closed discourse, although
it attempts to be consistent in its development.
Thus it is open to critique from other positions
which take the same historico-materialist discourse
as their base.

FOOTNOTES

1. By discourse, we mean the social production
of meaning which is the condition of any social
practice.
2. No claim of 'scientificity' or 'scientific
socialism' would make one more 'true' than another,
as much as it does not make any bourgeois discourse
'true knowledge'. On the question of the epistemological status of the historico-materialist
discourse, see R. Keat (1979) and G. Fahrenkrog
(1979).
3. The incorporation of certain discourses of
a popular nature, and which are part of the socialist discourse, into the bourgeois hegemonic
discourse (rent, regional inequalities, participation
in regional planning, etc.) are worth analysing since
they might help us to understand the specific working
of the discourse and its role in the reproduction of
the social relations.
4. These points were at the centre of the
political debate in the early 1900s. The Lenin-
Luxemburg or the Austrian Marxists' formulations
against Lenin's theory of the organisation of the
working class are some of the points. The ideological (?) dominance of the third international right
up to the sixties left this point simply out of the
debate since who would question the self-appointed
vanguard of the proletariat? Only in the seventies,
and as a result of the critique of 'real socialism',
has this point returned to the field of discussion.
Some of the more recent contributions from widely
different angles have been produced by Mandel,
Althusser, Baro and Carrillo.
5. One should note that Lenin refers to classes
as groupings of people with a common place in the

system of social production, and not to a thing in itself. This is logically consistent with Marx's definition of his 'guiding principles' (historical-materialism) when he says: "In the social production of their existence, men inevitably enter into definite relations, which are independent of their will, namely......etc." Both, Marx and Lenin, are referring to people or human individuals in their discourses.

The recent and very particular interpretations of that discourse made by Cuttler, Hindess and Co. (1977), in which they define agents as non-human entities, thus only indicative of 'places' in social relations, change the concept of class with serious consequences for the Marxist discourse (e.g. capitalist class without capitalists). The discordance of both discourses make it impossible to call their discourse a Marxist one, since by violating its own foundation, it ceases to be part of it.

6. In Fahrenkrog (1979), we developed a number of concepts to analyse social formations with other dominant modes of production and the effect the social relations have on the organisation of space.

REFERENCES

Bettelheim, C. (1976), Economic Calculation and Forms of Property, Routledge and Kegan Paul, London

Carney, Hudson, Ive and Lewis (1975), 'Regional Underdevelopment in Late Capitalism: A Study of the North East of England' in I. Masser (ed.), Theory and Practice in Regional Science, Pion, London

Castells, M. (1977), The Urban Questions, Edward Arnold, London

Cutler, Hindess, Hirst and Hussain (1977), Marx's Capital and Capitalism Today, Vol. I-II, Routledge and Kegan Paul, London

Fahrenkrog, G. (1979), Theories Concerning the Organisation of Space, Ph.D. thesis submitted to Cambridge University

Harvey, D. (1973), Social Justice and the City, Edward Arnold, London

Hechter, M. (1975), Internal Colonialism: The Celtic Fringe in British National Development 1536-1966, International Library of Sociology, Routledge and Kegan Paul, London

Holland, S. (1976), Capital vs the Region, Macmillan Press

Keat, R. (1979), 'Scientific Socialism: A Positivist
    Delusion?', <u>Radical Philosophy</u>, No. 23, 1979,
    pp. 21-23.
Laclau, E. (1977), <u>Politics and Ideology in Marxist
    Theory</u>, NLB, London
Leijten, Fahrenkrog (1978), <u>Lokatie van Onderneming-
    en en Ruimtelijke Planning</u>, le rapport,
    Geografisch en Planologisch Instituut, Kathol-
    ieke Universiteit Nijmegen, mimeo.
Leijten, J. (1980), <u>Ideology, Politics and Planning</u>,
    in this volume
Lipietz, A. (1977), <u>Le Capital et Son Espace</u>,
    Maspero, Paris
Lojkine, J. (1976), 'Contribution to a Marxist Theory
    of Capitalist Urbanization' in C. Pickvance
    (ed.), <u>Urban Sociology:Critical Essays</u>,
    Tavistock, London
Massey, D. (1978), 'Regionalism: Some Current Issues',
    <u>Capital and Class</u>, No. 6, 1978, pp. 106-123
Massey, D. (1979), 'In What Sense a Regional
    Problem?', <u>Regional Studies</u>, Vol. 13, pp. 233-
    243
Radice, H. (ed.), (1997), <u>International Firms and
    Modern Imperialism</u>, Penguin Books, London
Sayer, A. (1977), <u>The Law of Value and Uneven
    Development: Some Problems and Possibilities
    of Analysis</u>, paper presented to RSA, Regional
    Social Theory Group, mimeo.

A THEORETICAL APPROACH TO CAPITAL AND LABOUR RESTRUCTURING

Katherine Gibson

Julie Graham

Don Shakow

and

Robert Ross

A THEORETICAL APPROACH TO CAPITAL AND LABOUR RESTRUCTURING

Introduction

The capitalist system today is undergoing changes of a fundamental nature. Regions of traditional capitalist industrial activity are now in crisis, and the form of capitalist penetration into the Third World is significantly altering; old forms of dominant industrial organisation and their associated capitalist class fractions are being challenged by international capital, which is showing new vigour and potency; most significantly, the labour force under capitalism is facing new methods of exploitation which are difficult to recognise and to oppose, due to the persistence of regional and national chauvinism, racism, and other forms of class fragmentation. Yet, despite their relatively radical nature, these changes in the capitalist system are in no way indicative of systematic breakdown.

The problem of structural change within a system which remains quintessentially capitalist presents certain theoretical difficulties. Marxian categories refer to structures whose counterparts in reality are far from homogenous and whose elements show continually changing relations of relative dominance. The capitalist mode of production as described in <u>Capital</u>, however, presents a classic, monolithic, and analytically rigid aspect which appears distinct from the variegated forms of capitalism in history. In our view, it is nevertheless essential to assimilate the changing qualitative nature of capitalism within an overall theoretical framework that retains the logical method of <u>Capital</u> as it addresses the laws of motion of capitalism in general. The argument which follows constitutes a preliminary attempt to develop such a framework and to establish its applicability to

phenomena of interest to students of regional transformation.

The propositions established by Marx in Capital
pertain to a capitalism stripped of many historically specific details. English capitalism of the
nineteenth century and Western capitalism of the
present day both embody such fundamental characteristics as private property, private capital accumulation, labour power as a commodity, and a working
class bereft of all means of production save its own
labour power. Insofar as the abstractions of Capital
rely on categories such as these, the propositions
derived from these abstractions will be generally
applicable. At the same time, categories associated
with the more particular variants of capitalism give
rise to propositions of more limited applicability.
These latter propositions are generated at a lower
level of abstraction and are characterised by greater historical specificity than those of Marx's
analysis of capitalism in general.

The propositions pertaining to capital and
labour restructuring which we will attempt to
delineate in this paper are of this more particular
variety. As a consequence, it is necessary for us to
go beyond the level of abstraction associated with
Marx's analysis of the capitalist mode of production
in developing the logical framework within which our
less abstract propositions can be established. In
particular, we need to identify the structural
differences between variant forms of the capitalist
mode of production at a level of abstraction which
is more historically specific than that of the
capitalist mode of production in general (see Table
1). We need also to understand at a still lower
level of abstraction the relations of dominance and
subordination between these variants, or submodes,
that constitute the theoretical category, social
formation. It should be emphasised that the
progression from mode of production (level 1) to
social formation (level 3) does not represent a
progression from thought to reality. Categories at
all levels are objects in thought; they are useful
insofar as they illuminate social reality and thus
potentially contribute to the organisation of the
working class. 1.

The development of the capitalist mode of
production has often been described in terms of
distinct periods, or 'phases of accumulation', which
have succeeded each other in history. Many problems
are associated with delineating these historically
successive variants of the capitalist mode of

Table 1: Levels of Abstraction in Marxian Analysis

Level	Associated Categories
1	Mode of production
2	Submode of production
3	Social formation

production. It is, for example, difficult to retain
a sense of the complexity of history, while at the
same time specifying clear disjunctures, or transitions, between one phase and the next. Our analysis
identifies submodes of production as structural
building blocks which at any time in the development
of the capitalist mode of production may exist in an
articulated relationship to each other.

While the capitalist mode of production shows a
consistent basis for accumulation rooted in the
distinctive capitalist relations of production, the
predominant mechanism of surplus extraction changes
over time. Submodes are differentiated on the basis
of those mechanisms of surplus extraction, particular
to each, which embody the fundamentally capitalist
relations of production. That is, the defining
feature of each submode is the particular level of
exploitation that constitutes the basis of capital
accumulation.

The three submodes which we identify are
(1) the competitive submode; (2) the monopoly submode; and (3) the global submode. The competitive
submode is characterised by the direct exploitation
of a relatively homogeneous proletariat whose wages
are reduced to the level of physical subsistence.
Subsistence wages are enforced by the presence of an
industrial reserve army, which stands ready to
replace those workers given to displays of militancy
or recalcitrance.

The monopoly submode, which finds its most
characteristic expression in North America, is based
on the bifurcation of the working class into two
distinct segments, termed primary and secondary.
Secondary workers are exploited both directly and
indirectly. In the latter case, monopoly capitalists
impose unfavourable terms of trade on small competitive suppliers and subcontractors, which in turn
requires that these 'satellite' firms pay their
workers at substantially lower levels of remuneration than those accorded to workers in the monopoly

firms. This represents, therefore, a form of unequal exchange.

Finally, the global submode is characterised by the heightened interregional and international migration of productive capital and the rise of proletarianised labour at the periphery. Actual or threatened capital mobility operates as a lever of exploitation both upon workers in the mature industrial regions and upon newly proletarianised workers in regions experiencing an influx of productive capital.

Although the defining element of the submode is its unique lever of surplus value extraction, other more historically specific elements may be associated with each submode. These include characteristic forms of productive industrial organisation, organisation of the capitalist labour process, ideological perspectives, political structures and allegiances, and geographical influence. It is important to recognise that the submodes do not occur in pure form but rather articulate with one another in differing ways. The articulation determines the social formation, a 'structure in dominance' characterised by the presence of a hegemonic submode which defines the principal lever of exploitation of the formation. 2. The value of this formulation lies, in part, in its ability to transcend the weakness of existing periodisations of capitalist development. The dominance of one submode does not preclude the existence of other submodes articulated in a subordinate manner. Thus, we are able to examine a succession of structures without 'phasing out' the remnants of an earlier hegemony.

The structure of the discussion which follows reflects a progression from the highest level of abstraction to the lowest. In the first place, we begin by examining Marx's fundamental theoretical insight into the operations of the capitalist mode of production, the labour theory of value. At the level of the capitalist mode of production in general, we define value and examine the contradictions surrounding its production which Marx identified as essential determinants of capital accumulation and systematic change. In pursuing analysis at this level, we review Marx's exposition of the relationship between value and price, highlighting its relevance to an understanding of the capitalist mode of production in general.

Proceeding to a lower level of abstraction, we attempt to show how the concept of value can be employed to apprehend the phenomenon of structural

transition within the capitalist mode of production.
We develop for this purpose a theory of the value-
price relationship as it affects individual economic
sectors during capitalist crisis. It is here, at this
lower level of abstraction, that the major portion
of our paper is focused. In our exposition, we
concentrate on the sectoral value rate of profit,
whose movements are basic to the capitalist crisis
mechanism. For heuristic purposes, we first explore
the process by which devalorisation engenders crisis
and consequent structural transition on the sectoral
level. Generalising then to the whole economy, we
show how declining sectoral value rates of profit
and devalorisation create periodic crises and widespread systematic restructuring of capital and
labour.

At a still lower level of abstraction, we then
focus upon the specific forms of capital and labour
restructuring which signal a transition from the
hegemony of the monopoly submode to that of the
global submode. At this level, we discuss the
political economic consequence of capitalist
response to falling sectoral value rates of profit,
focusing upon the new position labour occupies in
regions affected by this transition. Finally, we end
with a review of the effects of the transition upon
the formulation of capitalist and working class
strategies, concentrating upon responses to the
current experience of older industrial regions.

Value and Price

We are seeking to understand systematic change in
terms of value categories because these categories
allow us to embrace the contradictions of the capitalist system. Marx's fundamental insight into the
capitalist mode of production was his recognition
that, though human labour reproduces the system
through the production of useful goods, the process
and product of that labour are controlled by a non-
labouring class. A system thus evolves that openly
acknowledges the property and exchange relations
which promote the interests of the dominant class,
but that obscures the basis of their wealth in the
labour of others.

Yet labour's essential contribution to the
reproduction of the system cannot be ignored;
instead it is submerged beneath the transactions of
everyday economic life, surfacing theoretically as
abstract labour time, or value. Value theory is the
tool by which we maintain and utilise the insight

that human labour fuels the capitalist system, and that capital alienates that labour from control over the system it reproduces. 3. A conception of value in its quantitative aspect allows us to perceive the way in which labour is allocated among the producers and the antagonists they serve, and among the capitalists who compete against each other in the process of capital accumulation.

Value as we have defined it embodies one of the two fundamental contradictions of capitalism, the struggle between capital and labour in the sphere of production. This fundamental contradiction, as it interacts with the intraclass antagonism between competing capitalists, generates the 'laws of motion' of the capitalist mode of production. In other words, capitalism is activated by two contradictory relations - that between capital and capital, and that between capital and labour - and the dialectical interplay of these two great contradictions produces the systemic dislocations that give rise to change.

This conception of capitalism is reflected in the terms of discourse appropriate to Marxian economic analysis. The competition between capital and capital and the struggle between capital and labour can be expressed in terms of separate analytic domains, which we designate the price and value spheres respectively. Clearly, in the operations of a capitalist economy the two spheres will interact, and in our view it is their interaction which generates change in the system. Credit restrictions engendered in the price sphere, for example, will have definite implications for the relations between labour and capital in the sphere of production. For theoretical and analytical purposes, therefore, it is necessary to establish some conception of the relationship between value and price.

The problem of the relationship between value and price has plagued Marxists for generations. 4. On the most abstract level, many theorists hold that the two categories must be related through some form of transformation, since surplus value is the origin, rather than simply the analogue, of profit. Yet on a day-to-day level, it is apparent that prices are determined by a variety of forces which have no direct relation to the labour time embodied in commodities. In an economy where virgin land has a price, and where investment in gold and ornamental diamonds vies with investment in the production of food and fuel, embodied human labour time and price seem quite divorced.

In our view, the separate spheres of value and price interact in a dialectical relation which is the basis for structural transition and, ultimately, for systemic breakdown. This proposition can be demonstrated at various levels of abstraction. In Capital, Marx develops at the level of abstraction appropriate to the capitalist mode of production in general the relationship between value and what he terms prices of production. The exposition in Volume III demonstrates how capitalist reproduction results from the reallocation of surplus value back into production by means of the distributional mechanism of capitalist competition in the price sphere. The value-price relationship as Marx develops it here is predicated upon a set of limiting assumptions appropriate to his analysis of what remains a highly abstract category, the capitalist mode of production in general.

Marx's purpose is to demonstrate the contradictory outcome of intraclass competition. In particular, he is concerned to show how the anarchy of competitive capitalist production undermines the basis of capitalist class power. In pursuing his exposition, he adopts the category of the general rate of profit, which allows the individual capitalist to share in the total surplus generated in proportion to his initial capital outlay. For any one firm or sector, the value rate of profit will not be equal to the general rate because the organic composition of capital varies on a sectoral basis. The formation of the general rate effects a redistribution of surplus value among capitalists in the sphere of circulation. In this context, Marx's analysis of necessity requires a transformation scheme between value and prices of production associated with the general rate of profit. This scheme has often been used by subsequent theorists as a statement of the relation between value and price. It should be noted, however, that prices of production are developed as a counterpart to values, and at a comparable level of abstraction, to indicate the distribution surplus. Prices of production, moreover, are long-run magnitudes. As a long-run category developed at the level of abstraction appropriate to the capitalist mode of production in general, they bear no determinate relation to actual prices. 5. Some criticisms of the transformation problem reflect a confusion on this point and incorrectly assume that Marx's formulation on this high level of abstraction is applicable to lower levels; thus, critics attempt to use Marx's abstract mechanism as an actual theory of price determination, and encounter a discouraging but predictable lack of success.

For the level of abstraction at which our theoretical discussion is being pursued, it is necessary to drop a number of Marx's assumptions while retaining one fundamental conceptual proposition: that capitalist competition in the price sphere tends to engender critical bottlenecks in the accumulation of surplus value. At this lower level of abstraction, then, we will consider value and price to be dual categories which are not linked by any transparent transformation; that is, the price and value spheres are relatively autonomous. Price depends ultimately on the distribution of income and is influenced by a myriad of other factors. Value depends on the relations of production and the outcome of struggles between capital and labour. It is not possible to infer a specific income distribution from a general theory of antagonistic classes. The relationship between values and prices is mediated through complex layers of transforming relationships, which must have a place in any theory that attempts to model the actual process of accumulation from one period to the next. Our theory is merely a first approximation to this, offering that first step of dissociating values and prices. For our purposes they are conjoined only through the dialectical process in which capitalist operation in the price sphere generates negative consequences in terms of surplus value extraction and capital accumulation.

In order to address these consequences, we will put aside Marx's concept of a general rate of profit and introduce instead a category which we have termed the <u>sectoral value rate of profit</u>. The equalising assumptions upon which the general rate of profit is predicated are not applicable at more concrete levels of analysis. Perfect capital and labour mobility do not obtain at the level on which our analysis is focused. The implication, then, is that rates of surplus value will not be equal across sectors of industry. This, combined with the variation in organic composition by industry which Marx discusses, means that value profit rates will show no tendency to equalise across sectors even given an increase in the mobility of financial capital.

It should be acknowledged here that our concept of a sector is rather vaguely defined. The concept basically reflects our view that, at any particular time, the economy can be disaggregated into various 'areas', dominated by a particular capitalist sub-mode of production (competitive, monopoly or global) and by a characteristic labour process which gives rise to a relatively uniform organic composition of capital and level of surplus value extraction. In the following section, we argue that capital allocation in the price sphere responds to movements in the differing sectoral value rates of profit, generating the actual form of capitalist reproduction and structural development.

We propose to use the category of the sectoral value rate of profit in developing a theory of structural transition between capitalist submodes. In confronting this rather difficult task, we first undertake the heuristic exercise of generating structural transition within a single sector before generalising the process over the entire economy. What follows, then, should be understood as an attempt to apprehend the dynamics of capitalism rather than an effort to elaborate a plausible account of the system's functioning in any partic-ular state of development. We begin with a sector dominated by the relations of the competitive sub-mode.

Structural Transition in a Single Sector

Within a sector of industry dominated by the competitive capitalist submode, the classical method of surplus appropriation obtains. That is, the process of proletarianisation strips the labourer of tools and other means necessary to reproduction, while the industrial reserve army operates to reduce labour's remuneration to the bare minimum necessary for subsistence. These are the mechanisms which facilitate exploitation under competitive capitalism.

The intensity of competition under competitive capitalism, however, may prompt certain firms within a given sector to introduce cost-cutting measures, technological innovations and, most importantly, methods of operation which increase the scale and intensity of production and facilitate the extrac-tion of relative surplus value. The introduction of these measures is necessitated by the capitalist's justifiable fear that a competitor will lower prices, thereby alienating from him the consumer demand on which he relies. Over time this process of innova-tion will tend to be replicated by most of the firms in the sector, generating expanded capacity.

In the course of expansion, however, a sector

may experience increased labour requirements, which may not be easily met through proletarianisation or recruitment from the ranks of the reserve army. The locality of the facility may be surrounded by fully proletarianised labour, for example; the supply of new labour may be constrained by national statutes, such as immigration laws; the economy may be booming, with the result that reserve labour is in short supply; or the technological innovations may require the application of labour in its more disciplined and experienced forms - any of these conditions could temporarily limit the access of capital to labour. As a consequence, capitalists in the expanding sector may be forced to wean labour away from employment in other sectors. Under these conditions it is likely that the favourable change in labour's bargaining position will promote a rise in wages above the level of subsistence.

The formation of labour organisations under these circumstances and the consequent upward pressure on traditional levels of subsistence does not go unheeded. Faced with the need to displace recalcitrant workers and to rationalise the production process in order to reduce dependency on human labour, competitive capital seeks credit assistance from the financial sector. To the extent that credit applications are successful, however, and living labour is displaced by dead labour in the production process, the basis for surplus extraction is diminished. Thus, while the fundamental threat to capital accumulation arises from increased bargaining power and associated militancy in the labour force, the most obvious response of capital - namely, the displacement of intractable labour with machines - offers no redress and in fact may aggravate the crisis of accumulation. This describes what Marx terms the tendency of the (value) rate of profit to fall.

It is important to distinguish value based profit from the experienced price rate of profit, and to note as well that the price rate of profit is the ostensible basis on which firms attract investment funds. Contrary to appearances, however, the price rate of profit does not provide the sole basis for investment allocations by finance capital. Under the heading of such broad qualitative categories as 'business climate' and 'investment risk', finance capital accounts for the efficacy of prevailing relations of capitalist production within a given competitive sector, expressed more precisely and at a higher level of abstraction in the sectoral value rate of profit. Thus, the assumption that finance capital's behaviour is rational purely in terms of price profit maximisation is misleading. Political economic considerations do in fact affect investment behaviour. A rumour of impending unionisation, transient declines in productivity, a change in government, are all as likely to affect investment behaviour as are purely 'objective' price data. The understanding such capitalists have of their own behaviour is itself ideologically mystified; the qualities of an 'astute' businessman, for example, are seen to be somehow the outcome of an ongoing process of social selection. But these primitive and casual observations reduce at a more abstract level of inquiry to the proposition that investment behaviour responds to a decline in the actual ability of capital to extract surplus value per unit of capital invested. That is, the credit sector responds to a fall in the value rate of profit within an industrial sector by withholding credit from the sector. We term the withholding of credit 'devalorisation'.

As a consequence of credit shortage, the competitive sector experiences over the short or medium term business failures, lowering of business confidence, underutilisation of capital stock and a high incidence of bankruptcy. This contributes to a process of concentration and centralisation of ownership on the part of the remaining capitals. The winnowing out of the least profitable firms necess- arily means that remaining firms have access to the entire amount of capital being allocated to the sector, even though this amount may be reduced below normal levels. Moreover, the sector is temporarily associated with high levels of unemployment and underutilised skills. In time, the reduced constant capital component in combination with a chastised labour force begins to generate substantial amounts of surplus per unit capital. But the effect of the previous crisis lingers in the form of greater sectoral concentration and an increased scale of operation on the part of each remaining firm.

Assuming an infusion of capital and the return to a healthy level of economic activity within the previously devalorised sector, the rising market potential of the remaining firms creates an increased demand for labour. Yet skilled and disciplined workers will not be impelled to leave existing jobs by the prospect of bare subsistence. Employed workers are recruited to expanding sectors only by the promise of better wages and conditions.

At the same time, the newly dominant capitals find
themselves less constrained by cut-throat competition to depress wages on a day-to-day basis. There
develops, as a consequence, a tendency for money
wages to rise in the course of capital concentration
(an ironic consequence since concentration itself is
the result of an attempt to forestall an increase
in labour's bargaining power). 6.

Under competitive capitalism, significant
increases in the price and value rates of profit are
constrained by the small scale of competitive
industrial activity and by capital's inability to
achieve ultimate control over an unstructured labour
force. In the restructured environment engendered by
sectoral devalorisation, these constraints no longer
operate to the same degree. Increased market power
facilitates investment in capital equipment and in
higher wages which promote more predictable levels
of productivity.

But concentration initiates new dangers to the
sectoral value rate of profit. With the rise in wage
levels, favourable levels of accumulation can only
be sustained by the alteration of the strategy of
exploitation. The structure within which a new
strategy is realised is termed monopoly capitalism.

The monopoly capitalist submode is characterised by a method of surplus value extraction and
appropriation dependent upon both a structured
labour force and market relations of dominance and
subordination among capitals. Labour force segmentation is here the fundamental mechanism of exploitation. 7. Segmentation of the labour force results
from the particular articulation of competitive and
oligopolistic firms characteristic of the monopoly
submode. 8. In the ascent to sectoral market power
and production dominance of concentrated capitals
during the previous episode of devalorisation,
larger successful enterprises establish relations
with remnant competitive firms. Often these small
companies are specialised suppliers of ancillary
production needs for the larger oligopolies. The
larger firms maintain their dominance by setting
market prices for commodities produced by the smaller competitive satellite firms and by entering into
temporary sub-contracting arrangements which allow
them to displace the effects of the business cycle
onto their dependent suppliers.

The labour force associated with the monopoly
submode participates in a structural market in which
there exist two distinct segments. The primary
segment of the work-force is generally organised and

is remunerated at a level higher than the common
standard of subsistence. Thus, excessive exploitation is mitigated by gains in money wages and other
achievements of organised labour. By contrast, the
secondary segment which is often associated with the
subordinate competitive firms and with certain
'unskilled' types of occupations within the larger
enterprises (e.g. clerical and maintenance work)
allows the dominant oligopoly firms full scope for
exploitation, directly in the workplace and indirectly via 'non-equivalent exchange' with satellite
firms. Differential rates of exploitation minimise
the contagious effects of organised class action; as
segments often coincide with other social divisions
- ethnic, racial, sexual - class cohesion is ideologically inhibited as well as economically impeded.
Segmentation is, then, both the product and facilitating mechanism of capital concentration. It allows
capital to absorb the impact of labour organisation
and increasing militancy by transforming class
antagonism into economic bargaining and conciliation.
Rationalising production to achieve a stable or even
shrinking primary labour force, monopoly capital at
the same time intensifies the exploitation of a
secondary segment still highly susceptible to the
encroachments of a growing industrial reserve army.
    Here too, however, the contradictions of the
capitalist mode of production in general activate
its inexorable laws of motion. Value rates of profit
within sectors dominated by the monopoly submode are
susceptible to decline just as they were under more
competitive conditions. The tentative achievements
of the primary segment of the working class, while
expedient for capitalists within the sector at a
proper historical time and place, pose a fundamental
threat to the value rate of profit and ultimately to
capitalist relations of production. As sectors
associated with the monopoly submode show indica-
tions of declining value rates of profit, devalorisation will operate as it did before, again generating a restructuring of capital. In the process there
emerges within the sector yet another structural
manifestation - global capitalism.
    Global capitalism is characterised by reduced
institutional and technological constraints on
international capital transfers. This permits the
expansion of the industrial reserve army on a global
scale, undermining the power of organised primary
labour and breaking down the segmented labour market
structure characteristic of the monopoly submode.
Capital perfects mechanisms by which it can migrate

and alights sporadically on scattered pools of
labour, escaping the turbulent waters of labour
militancy in one place and gravitating towards a
more tractable political environment in another.

As devalorisation takes place in industrial
sectors dominated by large monopoly firms, these
firms are no longer able to further the process of
horizontal and vertical integration in the context
of a single sector. Further access to credit is
predicated on the initiation of activity outside the
sector undergoing devalorisation. As a consequence,
firms proceed to engage in mergers and acquisitions
resulting in the formation of conglomerates which
operate in multiple sectors. 9. Submodal transition
thus brings about conditions extending well beyond
the sector of origin.

Structural Transition and Periodic Crisis

Our discussion thus far has proceeded in a bounded
environment, that of a single sector. While the
identification of structural transition at the
sectoral level may offer some interesting insights,
it does not in itself provide the basis for positing
transition from the hegemony of one submode to that
of another in the social formation as a whole. To
what extent, for example, are transitions in dominance in a given industry replicated throughout the
economy? We suggest that such transitions and the
convulsive circumstances of their birth do involve a
significant number of sectors. The episodes of
transition are therefore noticeable economic, social
and political events; and, in fact, they can be
associated with the phenomenon of conjunctural
crisis.

In other words, we have demonstrated that the
tendency for sectoral value rates of profit to fall
and the responsive processes of devalorisation and
capital reallocation generate submodal transitions
within sectors and that such transitions are associated with structural changes in the organisation of
capitalist enterprise and the predominant mechanisms
of exploitation. We have yet to demonstrate how these
tendencies produce periodic conjunctural crises of
widespread regional and national significance within
the capitalist system. In order to pursue this line
of inquiry we are compelled, at this point in our
formulation, to widen our analysis to include a
number of sectors within a social formation.
Descending to this more concrete level of analysis,
we must begin to examine the implications of deval-

orisation in one sector for the economy as a whole.

The extension to the economy as a whole prompts a closer examination of the inner workings of finance capital and the transition to the hegemony of global capitalism elaborated above. As finance capital backs away from sectors with declining value rates of profit, investment is withdrawn or requests for capital are denied in the process we have termed devalorisation. Even during crisis periods, funds liberated through the process of devalorisation will be diverted for new uses. Thus, for example, finance capital diverts liquid resources into a range of new activities, both productive and unproductive, offering favourable rates of return. New investment flows to sectors associated with commercial activity as well as with such unproductive activity as national defence. In the transition to global capitalism there is also a significant diversion of funds into direct foreign investment. 10.

Central to our argument, however, is the proposition that this reorientation of financial resources decidedly does not favour sectors in which the monploy capitalist submode is dominant. The reluctance of finance capital to valorise one monopoly sector at the expense of another can be understood in terms of the considerations which we have associated with the value rate of profit. Finance capital, for example, is repelled by the prospect of a contagion of labour militancy across sectors that are in fact linked by avenues of labour mobility or are perceived to be so by investors. The social reality of working class organisation is such that capital, in escaping the gains of labour in one sector and their expression in declining value rates of profit, will not willingly provide the basis for a similar victory in another sector. In other words, were capital reallocated within the affected submode, labour - insofar as it is mobile and its orientation to struggle is contagious - would precipitate similar crises of accumulation in newly valorised sectors. The result is that capital is effectively forced to devalorise not merely in one sector but simultaneously in all sectors linked by a common submodal structure and associated mechanisms of exploitation. This precipitates a number of simultaneous sectoral transitions whose conjunction is experienced by the economy as a significant crisis. This new type of crisis, in contrast to crises marking the transition between competitive and monopoly submodes, effectively destroys the market power of monopolies in the devalorised

sectors and consolidates the ascendancy of global
forms of industrial organisation and labour exploitation.

The impacts of periodic crises have distinct
spatial implications related to the geographical
extent of the social formations undergoing structural change. Crises within social formations dominated
by the competitive submode are relatively localised
in space; yet their occurrence gives rise to the
emergent dominance of the monopoly capitalist submode with its associated nationally oriented social
formations. In the crises of monopoly-dominated
social formations we witness the increasing
geographical scope of even relatively minor economic
fluctuations. In fact, throughout the history of
capitalist development progressive expansion in the
scope and scale of periodic crises appears to be
rooted in structural considerations. 11. Having made
this observation, we propose to engage a specific
instance of crisis and structural transition at a
still lower level of abstraction. In the concluding
pages of this section, we address a contemporaneous
and highly visible example of transitional conjuncture, namely, the crisis and restructuring of
capital and labour accompanying the emergent
hegemony of the global submode.

Capital and Labour Restructuring in the Transition to Global Capitalism

The ascendancy of the global submode over the
monopoly submode is accompanied by changes in the
delineation of hegemonic structures within social
formations. The current transition is marked by
changes in the role of the nation state, the political expression of monopoly-dominated social formations, and the development of incipient transnational political institutions. Although these
political and ideological aspects of structural
change are centrally important to an analysis at the
level of the social formation, we will focus in the
following discussion primarily upon the economic
aspects of transition, that is, those concrete
processes by which capital and labour restructuring
take place at the economic level. Our exposition
concentrates primarily on the North American
experience of the current transition from monopoly
to global capitalist hegemony.

As defined by Massey, among others, capital
restructuring involves a "reorganisation of the
ownership of capital". 12. The development of the

monopoly submode implies classic capital restructuring in the form of concentration and centralisation. By contrast, the emergence of the global submode gives rise to dominant forms of industrial organisation which are more complex and whose tendencies are less determinate. In particular, the envisioned transition to global capitalist hegemony suggests a return to a more competitive market situation which arises as a consequence of the incursion of conglomerates into the international arena.

The broadened geographical scope of conglomerate activity is heralded by the increased international involvement of financial firms. While the activities of finance capital have always had an international dimension, in the monopoly-dominated social formation this dimension was traditionally subordinate to, and contingent upon, developments within the framework of the national economy. Banks existed primarily to mobilise capital for production enterprises within their territorial range, which was seldom global in extent. The crisis of monopoly capitalism, however, has wrought significant changes in the role and function of financial institutions and has elevated the international dimension to a position of prominence. This is in part a consequence of the valorisation which follows on the heels of sectoral devalorisation in the monopoly submode. As the liquidity of finance capital increases, financial interests seek out investment targets abroad, including areas in which the 'contagion' of labour militancy has yet to spread. For example, U.S. banks abetted by recent liberalisations in laws governing banks and banking (e.g. the Bank Holding Company Act of 1956), have greatly increased their direct lending abroad. The largest U.S. banks now derive more than half their total earnings abroad; Citicorp, for example, earned 62 percent of total profits abroad in 1974 and, by 1977, the figure had climbed to 83 percent.

The growth of international activity reflects a more fundamental change in the role of financial institutions. Banks, which formerly operated to allocate capital inter-sectorally, are now the instrumentality which facilitates the spatial mobility of productive capital. Thus, they function as the underpinning of the exploitation mechanism under global capitalism.

The extensive forays of finance capital into the international arena have promoted corresponding developments in the sphere of production. This is reflected in the growth of the transnational corporation (TNC). The TNC conjoins the realms of transnational finance and transnational production, though generally subordinating the requirements of production to the imperatives of finance. Typically, the TNC assumes the form of a multisectoral conglomerate. Unlike oligopolies operating in the product and factor markets of a single sector, conglomerate firms do not pursue the traditional strategy of enhancing market power through horizontal and vertical integration; rather, through the processes of acquisition and divestment, they operate to maximise liquidity and the ability to mobilise capital for profitable investment. High profits are thus a function of flexibility and access to cash rather than market power.

Conglomerate firms are in the business of buying and selling businesses. They are engaged in accumulating and allocating surplus derived from the productive activity of their subsidiaries in accordance with rates of return around the globe. In subordinating production to finance, such companies become relatively independent of the vagaries of any particular product market. From the standpoint of the regional problematic, the significant characteristic of the transnational conglomerate is its role in facilitating interregional and intersectoral capital mobility and in dissolving the ties of productive capital to specific regional and national economies.

The emergent hegemony of the global submode is also reflected in the formation of international bureaucratic alliances designed to oversee and regulate the movement of capital across the globe. The IMF and World Bank have become the watchdogs of global capital investment, alternatively directing or restricting investment flows, mindful of the class interests of the global capitalist fraction. The Trilateral Commission, an association of prominent international capitalists, has accelerated the production of ideology designed to support the movement towards global enterprise. Such an ideology veils the direct activity of military or counter-intelligence agents in support of repressive nationalist military regimes that provide a propitious environment for productive investment.

The increased capital mobility gained through industrial reorganisation is a direct agency in labour restructuring. By labour restructuring, we refer to changes in the structure of the labour force, in this case the breakdown of the segmented labour market which prevails under the hegemony of monopoly capitalism.

The process of labour restructuring is promoted by the acceleration of such processes as deskilling, the fragmentation of production into various separable facets, and the replication of identical production facilities at different locations. Under conditions of heightened capital mobility, the need to mobilise workers rapidly in response to capital movements precludes the imposition of extensive skill requirements or elaborate job training programmes. The ongoing process of deskilling, in which the skill formerly embodied in the worker is designed into the machine, is therefore accelerated during the transition to global capitalism. Deskilling reflects the real subsumption of labour to capital as full knowledge of the production process is stripped from the worker engaged in existing production processes and replaced by new, more fragmentary skills, or withheld from labour entirely as in the case of newly developing fields of production. As Braverman points out, deskilling makes workers more inter-changeable and replaceable, decreasing capital's dependency on particular groups within the labour force or on the skills concentrated in the labour force of any particular region. As such, the deskilling tendency facilitates the consolidation of global capitalism, liberating restructured capital from production processes which involve the utilisation of a highly particular, skilled labour force in regions with a tradition of labour militancy, and allowing the use of labour at higher and more uniform rates of exploitation.

In addition to deskilling, the labour process has been restructured by the fragmentation of production into separable components. In the past, the tendency has been to concentrate all facets of a production process under one roof or at least in one region for the sake of reducing production time and transport costs. 13. Over time, however, the friction of distance has been somewhat eased by technological developments, and the magnitude of costs of production associated with transport of components has diminished relative to the cost of labour, which has risen due in part to the regional concentration of industry. Some firms have therefore broken down the production process into multiple facets in which such operations as research and development, fabrication, parts assembly, final assembly, warehousing and distribution are assigned to different facilities located in different regions or nations. Thus rather than specialising in

separate industries, regions and regional labour
forces now show a tendency to become associated with
particular operations. For the purpose of global
capital such a tendency fosters a corresponding
fragmentation in labour organisation and erodes the
traditional bargaining power of a regional labour
force.

Capital mobility has also assumed innovative
forms such as parallel production or second sourcing
which allows the multi-national corporation to exert
pressure on the rate of exploitation by operating
two identical production processes in different
locations. This strategy permits a firm to offset
disruption in one plant by overtime operation at
the other, enhancing the flexibility of capital
and increasing the vulnerability of labour.

As a consequence of these and other accompaniments of labour restructuring, a new international
division of labour is evolving, one in which labour
faces significant obstructions to successful
organising. Within the mature industrial regions
characterised by a history of labour organisation,
the labour force associated with dominant monopoly
sectors is being progressively undermined. In
response to declining value rates of profit monopoly
enterprises restructure their organisation,
diversifying into conglomerate activity and, simultaneously, entering into internationally based
production. This leaves the primary segment in a
severely weakened position. For example, in the U.S.
automobile industry, G.M. and Ford's exclusive
involvement in operations centred in Detroit has
been offset by the orchestration of a 'world car'.
The 'American automobile' has thus given way to an
automobile which incorporates a melange of components produced in many different nations.

Capital mobility has given capital a new
strategic lease on life. The very prospect of
regional capital outflow alters the bargaining
equation significantly in favour of capital and thus
provides a new and more effective lever of exploitation. As a result, the heretofore segmented labour
force in the older industrial economies is experiencing a process of 'secondarisation'. As capital
withdraws from the mature regions, the economic base
of segmentation collapses and the primary segment is
reduced to the level of the secondary labour force.
Unemployment is increased and those jobs available
are characterised by lower wages, job instability
and inferior working conditions. Along with the
secondarisation associated with contraction of

employment potential in the devalorised monopoly
sectors, labour in other 'growth' areas of the
mature economy is experiencing secondarisation
through the classic effects of deskilling and technological change. Within white collar occupations,
a shrinking number of skilled workers is juxtaposed
to a growing mass of semi-skilled clerical workers,
typically women, occupying increasingly routinised
jobs which offer low rates of pay. In addition,
declining regions are experiencing the revitalisa-
tion of small competitive capitalist firms, often
engendered by state policies designed to assist the
declining regional economy. 14. Such firms are the
locus of employment for immigrants and illegal
aliens whose status is insecure and who are offered
no legal platform for organising.

Thus, workers in old monopoly-dominated regions
are experiencing increasing rates of exploitation as
the size of the industrial reserve army grows,
exerting pressure on the stability of employment and
levels of wage remuneration. State assistance in
meeting the costs of social reproduction is also
withdrawn as the crisis of transition heightens
contradictions between the state's involvement in
facilitating regional investment and the provision
of social services. In the wake of capital movements, unemployment is increasing in the primary
segment and employment is growing among secondary
workers, including unskilled and traditionally non-
unionised workers such as women, illegal aliens, and
temporary immigrants. This development is beginning
to undermine the gains of labour under the monopoly
capitalism.

A corresponding process of labour restructuring
is underway on the periphery, which global capital
finds particularly attractive in its flight from
sites of successful labour struggle in the core.
Under the dominance of monopoly submode, Third World
nations were viewed mainly as the sources of vital
raw materials for nationally based oligopolies.
Under the emergent hegemony of the global submode,
however, investment in the Third World is increasingly directed toward manufacturing activity for
two specific purposes: (1) the provision of a
production apparatus to promote import substitution,
servicing the domestic market under the aegis of
foreign-based TNCs, and (2) the development of
export platforms. 15.

The deskilling and fragmentation of complex
production processes has contributed in particular
to the development of the latter. Export platforms

import partially finished goods, perform upon them some specific operation (e.g. assembly of electronic circuits), and then re-export them to the country of origin where they will be finished and sold. This arrangement enables foreign capital to take advantage of a favourable industrial climate: low wages, constraints upon unionisation, high productivity, and a politically enforced compliance with the institution of very advanced technologies.

Recent institutional developments in the U.S. have also facilitated the growth of export platforms. Articles 806.30 and 807.00 of the U.S. tariff code specify that tariff duties are to be assessed only on the value added component of goods imported into the U.S. That is, where goods are originally exported from the U.S. in a preassembled form and assembled abroad, the value of the unassembled components is excluded from import duties.

The export platform nations themselves have proved obliging. Mexico now has about 500 so-called 'in-bond' plants - including facilities owned by General Motors and Chrysler - which are exempted from Mexican import duties. Total employment in these plants is 110,000 workers, the majority of them women in their twenties engaged in assembly work. Typically labour in such regions is newly proletarianised and social reproduction functions are subsidised by a peasant mode of production. This enables the payment of extremely low wages.

The political economic consequences of export platform growth are pervasive. Note, for example, that China has made the most recent bid for export platform status, signing nearly 200 contracts to process or assemble electronic products for foreign companies.

In conclusion, the ascendancy of the global submode has contributed to the evolution of a new international division of labour. On this new terrain capital and labour confront each other in a radically altered strategic context, a context in which working class strategies are often baffled by the shifting hegemony of capitalist class fractions. We offer this paper as a preliminary attempt to understand the structural dynamics of recent systemic change under capitalism.

FOOTNOTES

1. Note that the use of 'abstraction' here differs quite markedly from that to which it is put by other Marxist theorists. For example, Fine and Harris (Rereading Capital, London: Macmillan Press, 1979) discuss a method of abstraction (Chapter 1) similar to the method of successive approximation used by Sweezy (The Theory of Capitalist Development, New York: Monthly Review Press, 1968). In both these cases, abstraction denotes purely logical concepts which are isolated from the complexity of the real world by a progressive filtering out of inessential phenomena. For Fine and Harris, the concepts of commodity and money are defined at the highest, most simple level of abstraction (p. 17). By contrast, the levels of abstraction developed in our paper denote levels of logical and historical specificity, such that the movement from level 1 to level 3 is a movement not only from simple to complex, but from the historically general to the historically specific; that is, from conceptions applicable over long periods of time to conceptions more delimited in their temporal applicability.

The process of mediating between abstractions and concrete, historical events is a dialectical one. The interplay of opposing forces in history suggests the raw material for abstraction. But statements and propositions regarding our abstract categories do not imply historical necessity. Such statements should indeed be serviceable to participants in the revolutionary process but they should not be construed as attempts to describe actual historical events.

For example, Marx identified within the English economy of the nineteenth century a structural relation of contradiction between intraclass capitalist competition and interclass capital-labour struggle. He abstracted this relationship from its historical context and defined it, at what we call the highest level of abstraction, as the fundamental determinant of the laws of motion of the capitalist mode of production in general. He demonstrated how this contradictory relationship could produce systemic breakdown through the tendency of the rate of profit to fall within the capitalist system as a whole. At the same time, in his discussion in Volume I of Capital of the concentration and centralisation of capital and the growth of the credit system, Marx hinted at the way in which this dialectical process could give rise to the emergence of new variants of

the capitalist mode of production - forms which we
are defining as submodes. Although he did not undertake an analysis of the laws and tendencies of submodes of capitalist production at this second level
of abstraction, he nevertheless provided materials
for such an analysis. In addition, much of the
illustrative material in Capital - concerning
primitive accumulation, for example, and the operations of individual capitalists and lawmakers in the
British economy - could be appropriated, at the
third level of abstraction, for a theory of the
articulation of modes and submodes of production
within the nineteenth century English social formation. In Capital, we have an example of the way in
which Marx's method proceeds simultaneously at
different levels of abstraction but focuses
primarily upon the highest level. Our task is to
show how this method can be extended, without
unwarranted inferences at inappropriate levels, to
an analysis of structural change at the level of the
social formation.

2.   In our formulation, we have adopted categories from Althusser (For Marx, London: Penguin
Press, 1969), but we have undertaken this theoretical
appropriation without accepting the Althusserian
conception in its entirety.

3.   Bell, P., "Marxist Theory, Class Struggle,
and the Crisis of Capitalism", in Jesse Schwartz,
(ed.), The Subtle Anatomy of Capitalism (Santa
Monica: Goodyear Publishing Co.), 1977.

4.   At present, the value-price relationship is
the subject of intense debate. The Cantabridgians
such as Robinson, Eatwell, Hodgson and, as a guiding
spirit, Sraffa, are the most avid supporters of a
position which views sceptically the analytic
separation of value and price. Opposing them are a
whole range of theorists who support Marx's conception of value and price. Fine and Harris (1979)
distinguish within this group the Fundamentalist
position exemplified by Yaffe; in addition, the
"Neo-Classical" Marxists including, for example,
Becker and Shaikh, adopted modified versions of the
classical position.

5.   Prices of production in Marx's formulation
are modified value categories and not actual prices.
Many Marxists have recognised this incongruity but
have persisted with the problem of the value-price
transformation at the level at which Marx addressed
it. Gerstein ("Production, Circulation, and Value:
The Significance of the 'Transformation Problem' in
Marx's Critique of Political Economy", Economy and

Society, Vol. 5, No. 3, August 1976) offers a critique of various theorists who attempt to 'solve' the transformation problem in Marx's terms but fail to criticise the formulation of the problem itself at its most fundamental level.

6. Harry Braverman (Labor and Monopoly Capital, New York: Monthly Review Press, 1976) relates the story of the strategies employed by Ford Motor Company in the early 20th century to both attract workers to the assembly line and control the 'quality' of labour that was accepted. One strategy involved the payment of $5.00 a day, which Ford considered an exorbitantly high wage; but as Ford himself was to recall it "was one of the finest cost-cutting moves we ever made" (pp. 149-150).

7. Our identification of segmentation as a method of surplus extraction builds upon the radical labour market segmentation literature in a relatively idiosyncratic manner. While we wish to acknowledge our debt to the excellent work of Edwards, Gordon and Reich, Vietorisz and Harrison, Bluestone, Doeringer and Piore, Rubery and others, our current work is based upon a critique of this literature which cannot be included in this text. The outline of our criticisms is found in Gibson, K., Graham, J., and Shakow, D., "Labor Market Phenomena and the Falling Rate of Profit: A Theoretical Prospectus", unpublished paper, Clark University, Worcester, Mass., 1979.

8. The industrial organisation characteristic of this submode has aroused much discussion amongst bourgeois economists critical of the overly reductionist neo-classical view of a homogeneous economy of competitive firms. The work of such writers as Averitt (The Dual Economy, New York: W.W. Norton, 1968) is notable in this regard.

9. This trend as it has operated in the U.S. economy is discussed and documented in Bluestone, B. and Harrison, B., Capital and Communities (Washington, D.C.: Progressive Alliance), 1980.

10. For a more extended discussion, see Baran, P., and Sweezy, P., Monopoly Capital (New York: Monthly Review Press), 1966; O'Connor, J., The Fiscal Crisis of the State (New York: St. Martin's Press), 1973; Becker, J., Marxian Political Economy (London: Cambridge University Press), 1977.

11. We would hope that our theoretical formulation will eventually aid in an analysis of long swings in the capitalist economy. One recent attempt to address this problem is Mandel, E., Late Capitalism (London: New Left Books), 1975.

12. Massey, D., "Capital and Locational Change: the UK Electrical Engineering and Electronics Industries", RRPE, Vol. 10, No. 3 (Fall 1978), pp. 39-54.

13. See Marx's discussion (Capital, Vol. I, Chapter 15) on the physical reorganisation of production associated with the rise of capitalist manufacture and modern industry for an anticipation of this mechanism.

14. A discussion of such policies and their role within the general framework of the global submode occurs in Susman, P., "Devalorisation in a Regional Setting: A Study of Northeast England", Worcester, Mass., Clark University, unpublished Ph.D. dissertation, 1979.

15. For a useful and extended discussion of export platforms see Trajtenberg, R., "Transnationals and Cheap Labor in the Periphery", in Zarembka, ed., Research in Political Economy, (Greenwich, Conn.: JAI Press, 1978).

IDEOLOGY, POLITICS AND PLANNING

A Reformulation

Jos Leyton

This paper is the result of many discussions with Gustavo Fahrenkrog and Ben Jansen and in the 'Werkgroep Ruimte en Politiek' in Nijmegen. Comments on an earlier version were made by Doreen Massey but mistakes remain the responsibility of the writer.

The discussions were directed to the question of a socialist interpretation and political strategy with respect to 'spatial inequalities' and 'regional economic and physical planning'. As a starting point, we were dissatisfied with Marxist studies which were restricted to the analysis of general tendencies in the development of contemporary capitalism or programmatic proposals that lacked a discussion of political strategy.

The problem posed was to develop a set of concepts which informs us not only that the driving force of society is still capitalist, but which also makes political calculation possible. In other words, we are not only interested in the so-called 'objective developments', but especially in the political relations that 'arise' on the basis of these objective developments. We hope that this paper is a step in that direction.

IDEOLOGY, POLITICS AND PLANNING
A Reformulation

Introduction: The Material Basis of 'Consciousness'

The aim of this paper is to develop some ideas which lead to an understanding of the mechanisms behind planning and the set of state activities (laws, money, regulations, planning documents, etc.) that help the organisation of space.

In general, one can say that the state has to be seen as a relation, based on and structurally permeated by the contradictions between classes in society. The different institutions and departments of the state manifest great contradictions. The actual working of the state is thus chaotic. It is the result of these internal contradictions; in other words, the reflection of the political relations between classes and class-fractions.

Classes and fractions rarely organise themselves as such. Class interests know many forms of representation and mediation in society. Individuals can formulate and represent their interests directly. But more often than not these interests are represented and mediated through interest groups, political parties, and organisations such as churches. Due to the number and complexity of forms of representation and mediation, it is usually difficult to distinguish a direct relation between, for example, a political party and the interests of a class or a class-fraction, at least in countries with a tradition in representative democracy. We would have to ask ourselves if a direct relation actually exists, especially as most agents do not represent their objective class interests in their political practice. The 'conservative' political behaviour of a great number of workers is a case in point.

To be able to understand state intervention in the organisation of space and, through it, to distinguish the class interests which are represented, it is necessary to tackle the question of political representation and mediation of interests, in particular the role of the political parties.

Let us begin to unravel the complexity of this mediation by discussing the position of the individual in society. To be able to reproduce daily living conditions, an individual (agent) has to establish relations with other people (relations of production). Activities and relations to other people are the basis of 'consciousness', ideas about those particular relations (Weltanschauung).

This does not mean that acts determine consciousness, but that such consciousness is the 'result' of daily experience and corresponds to lived conditions. It means that conditions can be experienced in different ways, depending upon the way the reproduction of life is organised. For example, somebody can think positively about his/her conditions and try to reproduce them, somebody else could experience them negatively and try to change them. The image or 'consciousness' is essentially defined in relation to the interest in reproducing one's life (self-seeking interests). Thus an agent will act intending to change, reinforce or accept his conditions as a result of the image which he/she has of them. Conversely, one can argue that these activities (change, reinforcement or acceptance) will influence the image an agent has of existing personal conditions.

> Men make their own history, whatever its outcome may be, in that each person follows his own consciously desired end, and it is precisely the resultant of these many wills operating in different directions and their manifold effects upon the outer world that constitutes history. Thus it is also a question of what the many individuals desire.... Everything which sets men in . motion must go through their minds; but what form it will take in the mind will very much depend on the circumstances. (Engels, 1968)

The idea which every individual has of his/her place in the world does not have to be consistent. Different aspects of life can be understood differently (e.g. work, nature, family, sexuality) and these positions can be contradictory, as can be his or her actions.

The conclusion of this short introduction must

be that one can hardly argue 'false consciousness',
when defining the image an agent has of his/her
living conditions, unless it is deliberately imposed
by conspiracy of, for example, some dominant
fraction of capital, which <u>consciously</u> establishes
its domination. In other words, Marxist theory of
ideology cannot be based on a conception of 'false
consciousness' as Poulantzas suggests. 1.

Equally, we would have to reject a reductionist
interpretation of Marx. In the Preface to <u>A Contri-</u>
<u>bution to the Critique of Political Economy</u>, Marx
argues that the relations (of production) which men
establish between themselves are necessary as well
as independent of their will. These relations
correspond to definite forms of consciousness. The
driving force of social changes is then posed, by
Marxist reductionists, as the contradiction between
the development of the productive forces and the
relations of production. The decisive role is,
however, the will and the consciousness of people
which determines their engagement in all social
struggle. Marx's political writings make this
position very clear.

A central focus for Marxist research must be
the ideas people have of their living situation and
their answers to the problem of reproduction of
their own lives. How does an individual's place in
the circuit of capital influence his/her engagement
in struggle? How do their ideas define their engagement in struggle and what are the consequences for
a socialist strategy?

An interesting argument that illustrates this
question is given in <u>Misrecognising Ideology</u> (Clarke,
J., 1977). The paper concentrates on a concept
central to bourgeois ideology, namely the concept
of the 'free individual' and the <u>objective</u> economic
base from which it arises.

The engagement in capitalist relations of
production means, for most people, the separation
from the means of production. In other words, there
is a dependence on the capitalist, or his representatives, who define labour, the forms of co-operation,
and so on. Workers are certainly not free at this
level. The capitalist is only interested in their
collective labour. There is no correspondence
between this relation and the notion of 'free
individual'. Clarke proceeds to argue that the
individualisation of agents <u>really</u> occurs in the
process of exchange of commodities. The basis for
exchange relations is the necessary <u>equality</u> of the
different parties, even in the most basic of the

exchange relations, the one between the labourer and the capitalist.

> Though Marx terms the wage, the exchange relation and so on, phenomenal forms, or forms of appearance, they are not, and cannot be reduced to mere illusions or errors on the part of the 'subjects' of these processes, whether we see these subjects as constitutives of these processes or merely performing the function of 'supports'. What we are dealing with are <u>real processes, real forms of relationship</u>. Agents do exchange, buy and sell, the wage labourer does indeed sell his labour and receive a wage in (equal) exchange. It is these relations themselves which are 'false', but false in a very specific sense - not as we have said, in the sense that they are not real, but false because they hide other sets of relations and processes of a very different quality and nature.
> ... not only are the 'appearances' real sets of relations but they are also <u>absolutely necessary</u> for capitalist production. The sphere of exchange is both the starting and finishing point of the process of capitalist production - the starting point, because it is here that capital in the form of money is exchanged for labour power and the means of production to initiate production itself; and the finishing point, because it is only with the exchange of the commodities created in the process of production for money that surplus value is realised. (p. 117)

In other words, the exchange between equals is a necessary element in capitalism, and cannot be seen as an 'appearance' of the 'real' production process. This is the basis of a necessary contradiction in capitalism: the freedom of individuals is opposed to the increasing socialisation of production; the increasing interdependence between individuals and the equal exchange between labour and capital is opposed to the basic inequality in the distribution of the means of production.

> What we have then is an analysis of a process - the circuit of capital - which is posited on a fundamental set of relations (those of capital and wage-labour), but which is divisible into a number of particular processes

> and corresponding sets of relations (production,
> exchange, distribution, etc.). Certain of these
> subordinate processes (those of circulation and
> exchange) involve relations and processes of a
> qualitatively different order from the fundamen-
> tal relations on which they rest (and which
> they serve to mask). (p. 117)

These different relations and processes form
together and individually the material basis for the
'consciousness' of people with respect to the concept
of the 'free individual'. Other concepts will have a
different material basis. But there is no straight
relation between the material basis and the images
people have to address this material basis. As
already argued, people are not simply determined by
the position they have in the process of social
production of their lives. There is no simple class
determination. Their ideas and their actions are
also subject to creative expectation and definition
in relation to the production of their own life.
(Brook, Finn, 1978.)

Class and 'Consciousness'

In the following argument, we will describe very
briefly how the process of mediation and representation takes place. The problem to which we address
ourselves is the relation between class positions
reproduced at the economic level, the struggle which
people engage in and over the state and the
ideologies, or discourses, which guide their actions.
In other words, if there is a social-economic
conflict, people perceive this conflict in a
certain way (ideology) and fight it out in a
specific form (politics). The first stage is that
people with a specific image of their conditions
'join' collective action, with the aim of reinforc-
ing or changing the perceived conditions.

> In the history of society, ..., the actors
> are all endowed with consciousness, are men
> acting with deliberation or passion, working
> towards definite goals; nothing happens without
> a conscious purpose, without an intended aim.
>
> .... That which is willed happens but rarely;
> in the majority of instances the numerous
> desired ends cross and conflict with one
> another, or these ends themselves are from the
> outset incapable of realisation or the means of
> attaining them are insufficient. (Engels, 1968)

This process of organisation for collective action
is the basis for 'institutionalisation' of actions
in organisations and of images in more or less
coherent ideologies. This condensation of individual
ideologies in institutionalised forms in its turn
affects the individual process of image formation.
In the same way, the 'images' of an individual can
be contradictory.

The formation of ideologies and images is, in
itself, not an individual process. It occurs in the
thought process of individuals, but is formed out of
the whole set of relations in which the individual
lives. The individual's place as an 'agent' in
society determines to a great extent his/her
experience. In this sense classes are an important
basis for organisation and collective action, not
directly, but through the thought and action of
individuals.

The actual expressions of institutionalised
ideologies are the different types of social movements, political parties, trade unions, pressure
groups, and so on. 2. It would be serious reduction-
ism to argue that these organisations and movements,
including their ideology, are determined by the
objective class position of the agents. In other
words, we cannot argue that classes (as opposed
poles resulting from the relations of production)
have a self-evident existence in the field of
ideological and political activity. As Laclau argues
(1977): "classes exist at the ideological and
political level in a process of articulation and not
of reduction". (p. 161) This means that ideologies
and the organisations which represent them, which
have their material basis in all possible spheres of
social life, can be 'used' by any class in its
ideological and political practice. Non-class bound
contents and concepts are the material basis for the
ideological class practice. Classes make a specific
selection of non-class bound concepts and contents
in their political and ideological practice. Laclau
gives the following determinant factors of selection.

> These ideological practices are determined
> not only by the view of the world consistent
> with the insertion of a given class in the
> process of production, but also by its
> relations with other classes and by the actual
> level of class struggle. (p. 161)

In other words, it is in the process of class

74

struggle that a class takes up elements which it can use to transform or improve its conditions. This argument of Laclau is certainly useful. It can help us understand a number of issues which, until now, were hardly discussed in Marxist theory. For example, it can help us to understand the transformation of social democracy from an ideology and political organisation of the working class to one which is also able to accommodate the interests of the more advanced forms of capital. Advanced capital, as a fraction of capital, was able to take over some elements of the ideology of the more qualified fraction of the working class. In the process, the content of social democratic ideology changed. We cannot argue that social democracy has developed from a party and ideology of the working class into a party and ideology of the bourgeoisie. But we can say that the political relations between classes are determinant by the 'use' of certain ideological contents and there is no conscious or conspiratorial development of social democracy.

This example, however, illustrates an important problem in Laclau's theory. He assumes the existence of classes in themselves and that it is classes which struggle at the political and ideological level. As was argued above, this is not the case since classes hardly ever organise as such.

Classes are groupings of agents with some common characteristics in the relations between them and to the means of production. In this way, classes are only defined in the Marxist discourse. From the point of view of Marxism, classes must be seen as abstract concepts that have to materialise in the thought and action of individuals. The Marxist discourse has thus to 'compete' with other discourses, a struggle which takes place in the ideological sphere. This struggle is essential to the political behaviour of people. A socialist strategy has thus not only to analyse the objective economic basis, but also to emphasise the analysis of the elements which intervene in the ideological struggle. We are not arguing that class-struggle should develop only in the ideological sphere. On the contrary, the struggle refers to struggle over specific economic and social problems. The actions of people, however, are determined by the way they experience these specific problems. And it is usually the case that experience in struggle produces change in thought.

Methodological Issues

The methodological consequences of this argument are
many. As we argued before, there is no other basis
for the images and world-views of individuals other
than their material life. The conditions and relations under which people reproduce their own life
can be manifold, even under the dominance of
capitalist relations of production. We have already
mentioned one of the factors producing these differences: the place the agent has in the circuit of
capital. There are many more: the relation to
nature, to machines, the place in the hierarchy of
an enterprise, income, housing conditions, trans-
mitted traditions, education, religion, and so on.
A precise knowledge of these conditions and relations is the main instrument for an effective
struggle in the ideological sphere. The aim of this
struggle is to produce a dominance of the historical
-materialist interpretation of social relations to
be able to change these relations. The position of
capitalists in class-struggle has necessarily to
coincide with their class-interests, otherwise their
conditions as capitalists would not be reproduced.
Workers can reproduce their lives without changing
social conditions, but at what cost?

To be able to transform social relations, it is
necessary that a majority of the people understand
social relations in terms of class-relations. These
do not necessarily have to be formulated in Marxist
terms. For example, the people/power-bloc or the
oppressed/oppressors contradiction has been
effectively used in populist struggles such as that
in Nicaragua. But, the struggles must be formulated
along class lines.

Some of these questions of research methodology
have been developed in the project 'Lokatie van
ondernemingen en ruimtelijke planning' and are
described by Fahrenkrog in this book. It is a method
which tries to develop a more precise and differentiated understanding of the structure and organisation of production processes.

An important limitation of this method is that
it concentrates only on the strategy of capital,
i.e. tries to explain the interests of capital. It
does not discuss the question of the interests of
the workers nor the ideological and political
expression of these interests. Furthermore, how
these interests are determined and, in turn, influence the strategies of capital is left unconsidered.
It is precisely these questions which we are trying
to answer. An example might illustrate further this

point: the location of General Electric Plastics in
Bergen op Zoom has had a substantial effect on the
local labour market and produced a very specific
group of workers, having higher wages than workers in
other industries, working in one of the most
advanced production processes of the world, responsible for handling highly dangerous materials, and so
on. This objective position defines to a great
extent their position in struggle (political and
ideological). One reflection of it is the low rate
of unionisation (20%). Another is their loyalty and
'esprit de corps' when confronted with an extensive
campaign against the environmental hazards which GEP
might cause and actually has caused. This particular
position necessarily has a strong influence on their
view of the social relations within society.

The knowledge of the position of the agents in
the process of production certainly constitutes the
basis of an analysis of the structure of the working
class. It is possible to determine their specific
relations to capital and to other workers. In this
sense, the above mentioned methodology is a starting
point. But there are other factors which present
themselves as objective conditions to the workers:
the state and its intervention in different spheres,
the housing question, consumer goods and service
availability and the tradition and world view trans-
mitted via education. 3. The connection between
these factors, the existing production processes and
relations is less direct. Although there is a relation between, for example, the housing question and
certain forms of state intervention and the strategies and interests of certain capitals, this relation
is usually not directly manifest. It is the result
of the combination of all the different forces
intervening, including elements of former stages of
development.

If it is necessary to analyse how the different
forces in society produce material conditions, how
they present themselves as objective reality and
form the basis of a worldview and conventional
wisdom, what research strategy are we discussing?
Most of the research in this field has been done in
so-called 'community studies', with the limitation
of an assumed unit (the neighbourhood) seen as a
totality of social relations. Such an assumption
makes the analysis of contradictions impossible.
(Brook, Finn, 1978) Research which attempts to
contribute to the development of political strategies
should, given the above argument of the role of
ideology in struggle, concentrate on the study of

the formation of conventional wisdom at relevant
conjunctures. One can understand this as an
'extension' of the method of analysis of the strategies of capitals to the interests and positions of
the workers in struggle. We would suggest that
'case-studies' could produce an important insight
into the correspondence between an individual's
objective conditions, his/her worldview and the
resulting economic and political actions. This type
of knowledge is necessary to develop a strategy
which intends to involve people in political
discussion and organisations. In the last few years,
there has been an increasing interest in this type
of research. The rediscovery of Gramsci's work and,
in a certain sense, the interest in Foucault's work
4. and the discussion of ideology are expressions of
this development. Castells more recent 'invitation
to a debate' illustrates our point. (Castells, 1980)

Hegemony and the Development of Planning
In the previous paragraphs, we argued that people
'come together' on the basis of shared world views
and experiences of problems, thus institutionalising
ideologies. This formulation could be interpreted as
a typical pluralist argument. This is so because
until now we have been speaking in abstract terms
about the forms in which people 'live' society and
the process of consciousness formation. Nevertheless,
in class society there is a continuous inequality in
the conditions of reproduction of people's lives.
This fact brings the question of dominance and
class-rule to the fore.
    In contemporary developed, capitalist societies,
the problem of perceiving a dominant class is a
difficult one. The concept of dominated or ruled
class is no less difficult to perceive. This is not
to say that classes cannot be distinguished. But
dominance and submission are hardly perceivable as
'physical' phenomena. The structure and the process
of class relations is a complex one and expresses
itself in many aspects of daily life as a reality
difficult to avoid. The dominance is expressed in
limits - in principle, the reproduction of the
social rules of the dominant capitalist system -
which are internalised in daily social practice.
To be able to analyse this apparently self-evident
class domination, Williams (1977) develops, based on
Gramsci, a concept of hegemony, in which the process
of 'internalisation' plays a central role. Hegemony
is, according to him, not simply a question of

ideological domination (which has a conspiratorial and manipulative connotation) but

> instead it sees the relations of domination and subordination, in their forms as practical consciousness, as in effect a saturation of the whole process of political and economic activity, not only of manifest social activity, but of the whole substance of lived identities and relationships, to such a depth that the pressures and limits of what can ultimately be seen as a specific economic, political and cultural system seem to most of us the pressures and limits of simple experience and commonsense. (p.110)

The material basis for this experience and commonsense are always the possibilities which people have to reproduce their own life, and those usually lie within the limits of the system of social relations. The necessity to engage in capitalist relations to be able to reproduce one's life, is thus for most people a 'natural' thing and is not experienced in terms of domination or exploitation. The hegemony of the dominant classes is a process which permeates many, if not all, aspects of life.

> It is the phase in which previously germinated ideologies become 'party', come into confrontation and conflict, until only one of them, or at least a single combination of them, tends to prevail, to gain the upper hand, to propagate itself throughout society – bringing about not only a unison of economic and political aims, but also intellectual and moral unity, posing all the questions around which the struggle rages not on a corporate but on a 'universal' plane, and thus creating the hegemony of a fundamental social group over a series of subordinate groups. (Gramsci, Prison Notebooks, p. 181)

The hegemonic assurance of the limits of the social system is not a static one. There is a permanent opposition and there is a continuous development of alternatives. The process of establishing and maintaining hegemony will always have to be alert to these transformations and react by controlling, transforming and even incorporating these threats to dominance. It is in this context that interest groups, political parties, pressure groups,

among others, form and develop. Their activity can
be very direct, aimed at a specific goal. It can
also be based on a wider image of social relations,
particularly political parties. The state is the main
point of confluence of this activity, especially that
of political parties. The state has thus a specific
role in controlling the limits of the hegemony. This
does not exclude direct action on the part of the
dominant classes when hegemony is threatened.
Gramsci notes, in a discussion of the dominant
capitalist class:

> It is true that the State is seen as the organ
> of one particular group, destined to create
> favourable conditions for the latter's maximum
> expansion. But the development and expansion of
> the particular group are conceived of, and
> presented as being the motor force of a univer-
> sal expansion, of a development of all the
> 'national' energies. (Gramsci, <u>Prison Notebooks</u>
> p. 181.)

As long as the process of hegemony is effective,
there is no possibility of threatening the dominance
via political organisations. Hence, there are two
possible courses of class confrontation: (i) A long
haul, building up a 'counter-hegemony' and (ii) a
crisis of the bourgeoisie which disrupts the hegemony. In practice the two will combine, a situation
in which the 'new' as well as the 'old' forces (each
operating in different directions) will be asking for
transformations of the social relations.
In most developed, capitalist societies, an
effective hegemony has been established for a long
time. One could almost argue of a 'consensus
society'. This allows the state to control effectively the limits of hegemony. Political struggle and
conflicts, in which the limits of the system of
social relations are discussed, occur mainly within
the state or are directed against the state. Most
political discussion follows the parliamentary road,
but there are other expressions of struggle which
interpolate the state directly such as squatters,
anti-nuclear movements and demand for abortion. This
is the dual context within which we would wish to
analyse the planning system of the developed capitalist countries.
The period after the Second World War is
characterised in the Netherlands, and other
countries, by the dominance of political parties
which move within the limits of hegemony: e.g.

social democrats, christian democrats and liberals. This period of effective hegemony creates the appearance of the existence of a "general interest": "a national popular, collective will, representing the hegemonic moment" (Hall, 1980). This general interest is the result of a 'common sense' which moves within the limits of the dominant social system. The planning system as it exists in the Netherlands is based on this 'common sense' idea of general interest. It is thus possible to displace a number of management-tasks to the state, because it is possible to reproduce the particular interests, mainly of different capitals, within the state. Through this mechanism, the planning system becomes part of the process of hegemony: it obscures the specific class interests.

We cannot agree with general statements such as: "planning is non decision-making" or "capitalist planning is impossible by definition" or "planning is an instrument of the bourgeoisie to control the contradictions which capital itself creates". Capitalist planning is possible, within the limits of an effective hegemony, not as a conscious instrument of the bourgeoisie but on the basis of the consent of a majority of the population. This does not mean that there are no problems in the intervention of planning in society. We will proceed to discuss two groups of problems, namely threats to effective hegemony and the impossibility of calculating specific developments within capitalist society.

1.   Effective hegemony can be temporarily endangered, as was the case at the end of the sixties. The main issue during that period was the discussion of the forms of rule. As a result, new forms of representation developed. It was intended to replace the traditional rule of an elite, bureaucracy and experts by rule through participation. This change in the form of hegemony had a major influence on the planning system: the creation of consensus had to happen through the planning system itself. Democracy and participation were keywords.

This lively process, for a certain period, certainly threatened the whole process of hegemony. The counter-hegemonic concepts developed by groups which worked in neighbourhodds, cities or on regional problems contributed to an instability. The formalisation and institutionalisation of participation was the means of re-establishing the hegemony.

A possible explanation of the struggle for participation and democratisation after 1965, the height of the post-war boom, was that the

'reconstruction-ideology' had lost its cohesive
function, and many groups began to press for better
housing, education or against the disruptive effect
of capitalist expansion. This does not mean that the
state apparatus had been placed in front of a new
task, but that some of the stages of the planning-
process would have to establish a new, and active,
consensus on part of the population. The changes in
the planning-system were thus not so much an
ideological operation, but the result of political
struggle over and about planning problems.

Another potential threat to hegemony was the
economic crisis of the seventies. But the hegemony
was so effective that it was possible to introduce
the idea of 'lower expectations' into the conventional wisdom, without any problem. This was
achieved not through conscious manipulation but
through the daily experience of plant closures and
unemployment combining with the existing elements of
people's conception of the world. The fact that
these ideas, which support the emergence of a new
hegemony, are also supported by working class organisations, allows the state to intervene in re-
establishing the rentability of capital. This meant
also a redirection of the planning system and the
dominant theoretical concepts which constitute its
basis.

In the Netherlands, it meant a displacement of
the so-called spatial deconcentration policy,
directed to promote the location of industries and
services outside the Randstad, by a policy directed
to the development of the Randstad. The WIR (Investment Act) originally designed, by the Dutch Labour
Party (P.v.d.A.), to promote the decentralisation is,
in practice, promoting investment in the core
(Harst/Klaver, 1978). In planning theory, one effect
amongst many others was to give a greater importance
to concepts like 'management of uncertainties' and
'flexibility of planning'.

Another threat to hegemony is presented by
political organisations which present strategies
which touch the limits of the system of social
relations. (Euro-)Communist parties and the Left,
within social democratic parties, have made policy
proposals such as nationalisation of large capitals
and constraints to the mobility of capital, which
actually would affect some of the basic rules of
capitalism (e.g. ownership and possession of the
means of production). 5. These proposals do not
constitute actual threats to capitalist society but
would affect the hegemonic system of dominance if

incorporated into conventional wisdom because,
at that moment, the possibility of affecting the
limits <u>is</u> real. As soon as this happened, there
would necessarily have to be a reaction to re-
establish hegemony either by controlling and absorb-
ing the political movement supporting it or as
necessary steps which capital would take to safe-
guard its position (e.g. capital flight, direct
intervention of capital in the political sphere).
There would have to be a necessary adjustment to
planning in those conditions. Many strategies of
the Left have failed to calculate the reactions of
the different social agents in a process of struggle
but this strategic assessment of capitalist opposition is at least as important as the formulation of
proposals directed towards certain problems of
capital.
2. A second set of problems, which cannot be seen
separate from the first, occurs because it is very
difficult, if not impossible, to calculate specific
developments in a capitalist society. Although every
capital has its own strategy, the result is dependent
on the strategy of other competing capitals. This is
particularly important to note if we intend to study
development at local and regional levels. Developments at these levels are so dependent on the development of specific capitals that the main function
of planning is limited to the creation of conditions
which make those developments possible, e.g. infrastructure, housing. And, even then, the actual
developments might be very different so that the
state ends up managing a 'fait accompli'. The planning of industrial estates in West Brabant illustrates this point. The waterfront was the object of
development of several plans for industrial sites.
They were drawn up under the forecast of an
industrialisation process which was either directly
related to the development of the ports in Rotterdam
and Antwerp or as a consequence of port development.
One of these areas was to be expanded almost four
times its planned size because of the expansion of
Shell Chemicals. Other areas were reduced in size
(e.g. Dintelmond) or, if developed, are still under-
occupied (e.g. Bergen op Zoom). One of the original
plans, the biggest one (Reimerswaal, 4000-6000 ha),
has been cancelled. On the other hand, actual
industrial development has placed heavy strain on the
provision of industrial sites in the cities and towns
of the interior (Etten-Leur, Breda, Oosterhout,
Raamsdonkveer). The industrial development of the
'60s and '70s has been mainly centred around the

production of consumer goods, specialised products for chemical and off-shore oil industry, industrial services, and so on. We can most certainly argue that, although plans were carefully calculated and some implemented so that an extensive industrial infrastructure was available, actual industrial development continued to create an uneven landscape.

In the course of the research on the location of enterprises and planning in West Brabant, we pin-pointed an important factor that underlay these problems. It relates to the difference between the dominant political ideas, the conventional wisdom about regional and local developments and the requirements of the different capitals and groups of capitals. Immediately after the Second World War, Noord-Brabant offered particularly advantageous conditions for the location of industries: labour was available, as a result of the expulsion of labour from agriculture, and access to the most important north-west European markets was easy. The major political parties in Noord-Brabant recognised these objective conditions. As Catholicism played a key-role in the dominant conventional wisdom, the response of the political parties was to argue that concentrated industrialisation produced large-scale urbanisation which in turn generated moral decline and anti-church positions. Hence, they argued, what Noord-Brabant needed was decentralised industrial-isation, i.e. the industrialisation of rural areas. 6. The result of this policy was that a number of small places (Oudenbosch, Rucphen en Etten-Leur) were defined as poles of industrial development and thus could access central government development subsidies. This policy has been a quali-fied success. Of all subsidised industrial sites, only 18% were still unused after 6 years (1952-1958), compared with 50% in other Netherland development areas. In this case, regional policy only strength-ened the existing tendencies of industrial location in West Brabant.

These early post-war plans, developed on the basis of the then dominant ideas, suited the strategy of but a small part of industrial capital. Capitals not so favoured also wanted their necessary condi-tions realised. Although the dominance of the Catholic world view decreased in the '50s and '60s, the regional state apparatus was not prepared to meet the needs of these capitals. Many of these industrial capitals came from the Rotterdam area or were closely connected with it. Massive growth in Rotterdam had produced a shortage of land and

labour. This led to an active intervention of the
Rotterdam planning authorities in the development of
industrial sites in the west of Noord-Brabant. The
Rotterdam Council had long been dominated by social
democrats and was better prepared to respond technically and politically to industrial growth. The
planning bodies of Rotterdam were actively involved
in the planning and development of the industrial
sites of Dintelmond, Moerdijk and Dombosch, mainly
to create possibilities for expansion for their
'own' industries, namely water transport, metal-
related and chemical industries. As this example
shows, the 'success' or 'failure' of planning is not
dependent on the internal structure and form of
capitalist planning itself, but on the politically
dominant ideology and the actual strategy of capitals
and all other social agents. The active involvement
of the planning body provided the necessary 'correc-
tions'; the intervention of Rotterdam did not generate many problems because of the simultaneous
change of the dominant ideology in Noord-Brabant.
This is not always the case: the central state might
also intervene in a repressive form, for example, in
the question of location of nuclear power plants
against local resistance. The resistance resulting
from locally dominant ideologies might nevertheless
succeed, depending on the issue and the balance of
forces within the national state.

Conclusion
We hope that this paper has succeeded in giving an
impetus to further discussion and development of
concepts which will allow for a more differentiated
analysis of state intervention and planning from a
Marxist viewpoint. We have argued that, in developed
capitalist countries, we cannot define the intervention of the state as a direct instrument of the
bourgeoisie. To do so, places us squarely in the
camp of conspiracy theory. Planning is even less of
an ideological operation to control and direct the
workers and working class movements. Capitalist
planning, in its contemporary form, is the result of
an effective hegemony, expressed in the existence
and experience within the limits of capitalist
social relations and based on the 'Weltanschauungen'
of most people.

FOOTNOTES

1. In his latest book, State, Power, Socialism (1978), Poulantzas also rejects this position.
2. We would have to reject the notion that it is the dominant class which provides the means of representation of the working class (via the state or any other obscure manipulation). The means of representation are the result of social and historical processes in which class hegemony plays a central role.
3. Tradition cannot be understood as a direct survival of the past, but has to be seen as a transformation of the past, in the sense that specific elements still exist and have a meaning in today's relations.
4. See, for example, Centre, Peripherie, Territoire (Paris 1978), in which several authors use elements from Foucault's conceptual framework, as well as Poulantzas (1978).
5. Für eine arbeitnehmerorientierte Raumordnungs - und Regionalpolitik, Köln 1977. The Alternative Economic Strategy advocated by many worker organisations in England.
6. Welvaartsplan voor de provincie Noord-Brabant (1947).

REFERENCES

Brook, E. and D. Finn (1978), 'Working Class Images of Society and Community Studies' in On Ideology, London
Carter, S. (1979), 'Class Conflict: The Human Dimension' in Pat Walker (ed.), Between Labour and Capital, Brighton
Castells, M. (1980), 'Cities and Regions Beyond the Crisis: Invitation to a Debate' in International Journal for Urban and Regional Research, 1-1980
Clarke, J., I. Connell and Roisin McDonough (1978), 'Misrecognizing Ideology, Ideology in Political Power and Social Classes' in On Ideology, London
Engels, F. (1968), 'Ludwig Feuerbach and the End of Classical German Philosophy' in Marx/Engels Selected Works, London
Fahrenkrog, G. (1980), On the Question of Method in Regional Analysis, in this volume
Gramsci, A. (1971), Selections from the Prison Notebooks, London

Hall, S. (1980), 'Popular Democratic vs. Authoritar-
     ian Populism: Two Ways of Taking Democracy
     Seriously' in Alan Hunt (ed.), <u>Marxism and
     Democracy</u>, London
Van der Harst, M.C. and J.A.M. Klaver (1978), WIR,
     een praktische toelichting, Deventer
Laclau, E. (1977), <u>Politics and Ideology in Marxist
     Theory</u>, London
Mercer, C. (1980), 'Revolutions, reforms, or reform-
     ulations? Marxist discourse on democracy' in
     Alan Hunt (ed.), <u>Marxism and Democracy</u>, London
Poulantzas, N. (1978), <u>State, Power, Socialism</u>,
     London
Projekt Ideologie-Theorie: Theorien uber Ideologie,
     Berlin, 1979
Williams, R. (1977), <u>Marxism and Literature</u>, Oxford

CAPITAL RESTRUCTURING AND THE
CHANGING REGIONAL ENVIRONMENT

Paul H. Susman*

* I am grateful to Phil O'Keefe for support during
this research and for comments on this paper.

CAPITAL RESTRUCTURING AND THE CHANGING REGIONAL ENVIRONMENT

Introduction

Regional problems persist despite a multitude of programmes and policies designed to counteract, if not eliminate and reverse them. In general terms, this failure to solve regional problems can be seen as a result of incorrectly siting regional problems in the region per se and not placing them within an understanding of the global capitalist system. The objective of this paper is to provide a perspective, derived from political economic analysis, on the process of devalorisation, or reduction in value of capital, both constant and variable, and to indicate associated changes in the regional environment. It is posited that devalorisation is part of a capital restructuring process in which the affected region is 'readjusted' to better fit into the international division of labour. Such readjustment entails major changes in the social relations of production and reproduction. Established gains by the working class are directly or indirectly undermined by this process of devalorisation.

Private capital and the public sector are both involved in the process. Not only are there direct economic and social impacts in this process, but also indirect and long term consequences resulting from the continuing production of nature both suited to, but simultaneously antagonistic to, the survival of the capitalist mode of production.

Theoretical Focus

In brief, the theoretical basis of the analysis presented here is derived from political economic insights into the capitalist system in which the central dynamic is the drive to accumulate capital.1. Accumulation, however, does not occur in a frictionless environment. Both intra-class competition and inter-class conflict generate contradictory tendencies that periodically surface within the system in the form of crises. 2. Intra-class competition between capitalists leads individual firms to adopt labour-saving technologies. While proving profitable in the short-run, as these innovations become standard over the industry, there may be a decline in the rate of profit resulting from an overall reduction in the total labour-produced surplus-value.

Furthermore, class conflicts between capitalists and workers arise over control of the product of labour at the most fundamental level, surplus-value, and over the labour-process itself. Such conflict can lead to technological changes in production as capitalists attempt to minimise their wage bill and conflict with labour, and this, in turn, may contribute to a decline in the sectoral rate of profit. While this is only a schematic of part of the dynamics of the system, it is important to note that both intra-class and inter-class conflicts create contradictory tendencies in the capitalist system that push it simultaneously towards expansion and breakdown.

Two tendencies resulting from these forces are summarised as two of the 'laws of motion' of capitalism:

> the law of the falling rate of profit; and the law of concentration and centralisation of capital. Like all laws, whether physical or social, these laws must be thought of as expressing tendencies, which, under given conditions might be counteracted temporarily by other tendencies or forces. 3.

In the face of a declining rate of profit, it is vital to the survival of existing capital to re-create conditions of profitability. Capital that is not reproduced and expanded at or above the average rate of profit is, in effect, partially destroyed. During crisis periods, accumulation becomes even more difficult and the rate of profit may plummet, more precipitously in some sectors (capital goods, for example) than others. 4. Small companies, unable to maintain their competitive positions during crises fold or are absorbed by larger firms, often based outside the immediate region. Thus, external control over local economies by extra-regional national or international enterprises tends to

increase during crises bringing with it an attendant
change in the industrial structure of affected
regions and concommitant impacts on the standard of
living and the basic social order of the region.
Regions with a high concentration of low-profit
sectors are more likely to experience significant
structural changes which serve to recreate conditions
for profit-rate restoration.

It is our contention that investment decisions
for restoration of the rate of profit are increasingly taken by financial institutions and transnational
corporations operating on a global scale. Furthermore, the current period of advanced capitalism, or
late capitalism, is qualitatively different from
earlier periods in three important respects:

1. Centralisation of capital is greater than
ever before, enabling transnational corporate profit
levels to surpass the GNP of many countries and
making entry into various industries almost impossible for small enterprises. 5.

2. The complexity of linkages, particularly
between production capital and money capital, sub-
sumed in the organisation of TNCs, renders state
controls over these institutions minimal. Transfer
pricing policies, double accounting procedures,
access to international and foreign financial sources
including Eurodollar and Eurobond markets, and the
ability to rapidly invest and disinvest sectorally
and geographically all contribute to the strength of
the transnational corporation. 6.

3. Further internationalisation of capital
includes both penetration into socialist countries,
evidenced in the number of co-production agreements
with TNCs, and establishment of manufacturing
production in the Third World. 7. This implies direct
and indirect capital outflow from manufacturing
regions in the First World.

The shape of the world economy is strongly
influenced by the relationships of national economies
to TNCs and by the changing role each national
population plays in the new international division
of labour. This theoretical focus provides the basis
for understanding why regional change in one country
is tied to the operations of TNCs that seek capital
accumulation on a world scale.

Devalorisation
Some of the ebbs and flows of the world capitalist
system are reflected in the fate of specific
regional economies where, particularly during the
crisis phase of the industrial cycle, profit

realisation proves more difficult. There are a
number of capitalist responses to crises including
not only direct capital outflow from the low-profit
sectors for investment elsewhere, but also devalorisation, or reduction in value, of specific capital
in order to create conditions conducive to future
capital accumulation. 8. Devalorisation processes
are a means of transforming entire regional economic
structures. While devalorisation is most apparent
during crises, it is a continuous process as industries and the capital associated with industries are
destroyed and renewed.

Devalorisation measures are not proportionally
or evenly applied in every industry or every firm in
the economy. Those industrial sectors which are
advanced, or advanced firms within particular industries, are not devalorised, or are only partially
devalorised. Conversely, those industries exhibiting
outmoded production technologies and a surfeit of
labour relative to more advanced firms, are subjected
to extensive devalorisation and may, as a consequence,
be forced to sell controlling interest to a competitor or, perhaps, financial institutions. Leading
(and usually the largest) firms are least affected,
while those of medium or low productivity are
hardest hit. By selectively devalorising firms
operating at below average levels of profitability,
new norms are established for prices and the social
allocation of labour. Firms that were once able to
capture surplus-profits or technological profits, as
a result of early technological innovation, now
define the average sectoral level of productivity and
hence, profitability.

Destruction of fixed capital by devalorisation
in the below-average firms and sectors absolutely
reduces the capital extant in the society. Combined
with lower real prices emerging from competition,
this may result in less available capital, but more
profitable conditions for future investment. This is
true for several reasons.

First, as constant capitals are devalorised
($c/c = q$ diminishes), any production that continues
is contributing to a higher rate of profit (P
increases as S' (1-q) increases). Second, higher
unemployment leads to less bargaining power for
labour, which may result in lower real wages (higher
S'). Third, a cheapening of commodities via competition preceding devalorisation results in a reduction
in the cost of labour subsistence and the wage. If
the consumer commodity package that constitutes the
wage is reduced in value, the amount of variable

capital investment for labour-power may be reduced. In effect, there has been a devalorisation of labour power and a consequent increase in the rate of surplus-value ($S' = s/v$) and rate of profit.

Reducing the value of capital by devalorisation is achieved in the price sphere by depreciating fixed capital holdings. Depreciation policies, often enforced by banks, respond to declining sectoral rates of profit. Thus, devalorisation processes are independent of individual capitalists, and reductions in capital value are as involuntary as the need to develop the forces of production and to maintain at least the average rate of profit. In devalorisation processes, the individual firm must have alternative sources of capital-expansion available and/or capital reserves must be ample to maintain the firm's capital in a competitive position. As a result, the impact of devalorisation will be least on large firms (such as transnational corporations) with larger capitals and access to credit from the same financial institutions that deny capital to smaller enterprises. 9. The consequent increase in the concentration and centralisation of capital is further amplified in each succeeding round of investment, devalorisation, reinvestment, etc.

Regions with high concentrations of industries undergoing devalorisation are likely to experience significant changes in the local economic structure and in the welfare conditions of the affected population. Over time, a systematic shift in investment would be expected, from older industries using more skilled labour inputs, to new industries using less skilled labour inputs. The older industries, with more organised and militant work forces, are the most likely to be devalorised. In response to low rates of profit, capital is directed to other sectors by financial institutions and TNCs. Included among the recipients of new investments are industries employing unorganised, newer (immigrant and/or illegal labour, minorities, women) and less skilled (or industries requiring lower skill levels) members of the work force. Easily hired and fired, trained and threatened, and receiving lower wages, the labour force in the new sectors is less likely to confront employers with demands for a greater share of surplus-value or for changes in the work process. The regional work force is peripheralised in this way. Its role in the international division of labour is maintained so long as more profitable conditions elsewhere do not supplant it. 10.

State Devalorisation

In addition to devalorisation of privately controlled capital, public sector or state capital may be
devalorised. As recurrent crises and barriers to
accumulation have intensified, particularly since
World War II, the state has engaged in practices
designed to promote private sector vitality. State
revenues, largely from taxation, may be allocated
to both productive and non-productive channels.
Productive investments will add to value in the
economy, while non-productive expenditure will ultimately contribute to a reduction in total capital
available for expansion and accumulation. 11. (This
may lead to a decline in the organic composition of
social capital and thus promote tendencies towards
profit rate restoration.)

State investment of devalorised capital is,
perhaps, clearest in the case of public industries.
These will typically be industries vital to the
economy as a whole, but difficult to operate profit-
ably without increasing individual capitalist's
costs, to prohibitive levels. Concentrated in power
generation, heavy industries, particularly those
facing stiff international competition, and, industries evidencing losing competitive positions where
the loss would be significant to the national
economy, such state investment serves to promote
private capital while sustaining the basis of the
national economy. Most examples of public industries
show low profit margins, or even losses each year. 12
This poor performance is allowed because of the use
of devalorised capital, or capital that is not being
used for its self-expansion at the average rate of
profit. Derived from surplus-value appropriated
through taxation, devalorised state capital is
invested with the expectation of lower than average
profit rates. While depleting the theoretical total
amount of surplus-value that may be invested at
average rates of return, it does assure increased
levels of commodity production and value production
despite possible crisis conditions. Furthermore,
without such state intervention, it is likely that
other industries may suffer due to higher input
costs.

State investment of devalorised capital in
infrastructure, necessary to private sector production and accumulation, is also a redistributive
mechanism by which the working class is forced to
subsidise private capital even further. Creation of
the conditions of profitable production and potential employment not only reduces costs of production

to the individual capitalist, but also further devalorises labour-power, generating increased dependence upon the state for sustenance.

Devalorisation of labour-power must be understood in its class context. From the capitalist class perspective, the private outlay of variable capital is reduced as some of the value associated with reproduction of the work force is provided by the state. Thus, possibilities of a higher sectoral rate of profit are restored as the rate of surplus-value is increased (see footnote 4). From a working class perspective, the ability of the population to sustain its economic security and social fabric is reduced to reliance upon a political state in which labour interests may be less directly influential than in the work place. In any case, labour induced demands for the state to positively regulate the private sector have little likelihood of significantly bringing about improved wage and working conditions.

Labour-power is further devalorised by state funding of housing construction and subsidisation of rents. While investing devalorised capital in rent-controlled residential construction, it once again absorbs costs that previously were incorporated in the wage. Collective consumption (by all taxpayers), via state action, of housing reduces the necessary wage level, supports construction work, and 'induces' population concentrations in particular locations. Depending upon which segment of the population is due to occupy the housing, the location may vary, thus permitting isolation, discrimination, and control functions to become intertwined with the legitimising public provision of low-cost housing.

State subsidy provision to private capital for meeting employment criteria, whether based on numbers, occupational categories, sex or nationality, results in a diminuation of the value of variable capital, i.e. another case of labour-power devalorisation. Direct subsidies per additional employee, for example, permit lower wage levels and/or a higher rate of surplus-value per worker. The additional surplus-value may be from direct exploitation at lower wage levels, or it may be surplus-value that has been appropriated from other workers and redirected by the state to the particular private sectors earmarked for subsidisation.

Thus, state devalorised capital expenditure is really the anticipated devalorisation of labour-power advanced to the private sector. The fundamen-

tal result of state policies is to bring the value
of national labour-power more into line with the
international division of labour-power. This is the
crucial factor for national economic survival - the
factor of attraction or repulsion of transnational
corporations - and the historically evolved means of
maintaining the capitalist advantage in the class
struggle.

The impact of state policies is not spatially
uniform, but concentrates in those regions already
suffering decline. New investment in these regions
will be concentrated in industries using up-to-date
productive technologies and offering suitable turn-
over and profitability. These 'modern' firms will
tend to be clustered creating a polarised landscape.
Location in industrial parks or estates gives firms
access to transportation and communication facilities as well as other infrastructure, and, in many
cases, it provides firms with highly subsidised
buildings and other amenities, through the implemen-
tation of state policies. Centralisation of capital
outside the region results in similar policies
determining new investment locations for different
capitals.

Polarisation is further augmented by devalorisation of entire areas housing 'inefficient' firms.
Just as production may cease in the extreme devalorisation case, so do areas cease as residences for
large unemployed populations. Thus, the concentration
of capital in production is reflected by the concentration of the population who have moved or been
moved closer to potential employment. Even as private
capital moves in to take advantage of subsidies,
infrastructure, and other forms of state devalorised
capital investment, the population of the affected
regions is being placed in more marginal conditions.
This dialectic extends as the vulnerability of the
population increases to changes in profitability on
a global scale. Thus, for the working class, the
ability to attain better economic and life-support
conditions is eroded away on two fronts. One is the
ability of private capital, particularly transnational corporations and financial institutions, to
change plant locations; move capital out of regions;
and, in general, to engage in devalorising and associated deskilling practices with respect to the
regional work force. The second front is the gamet
of state policies, undermining the value of labour-
power, even as the state performs, in some cases,
legitimation functions.

Contradictions are inherent in the use of

devalorised capital by the state. Not only may unproductive state expenditure contribute to existing problems for the capitalist class, but state devalorised capital investment results in a qualitative change in social relations of production; part of the continuing integration of the working class into the new international division of labour.

Capital restructuring not only creates conditions for higher private sector profitability as production relations are changed, but it also causes changes in the social relations of production. Options that once existed and framed the basis of social existence and continuity are removed and replaced by less discretionary and increasingly commodified forms of interaction.

Such changes are reflected in residential locational shifts in accordance with provision of employment opportunities and new or available housing. Furthermore, in areas with a restructured industrial base, changes also occur as more women enter the wage labour-force and increasingly occupy the 'deskilled' job categories that replace the formerly male dominated 'higher skill' jobs. Unemployment in the traditional industries combined with lower wages in the new jobs may result in a decline in family incomes. Other social changes also occur as a result of the new population dynamics. Social patterns of interaction are necessarily transformed as the fabric of neighbourhoods is unravelled by steady outmigration. Collective provision of childcare and other reproductive functions that may be a function of family and friendship networks are replaced by commodities or services-for-pay. The fundamental ability of a population to provide for its own needs is destroyed as it is increasingly moulded to serve the machines of restructured capital.

One outcome of the devalorisation and capital restructuring process is a change emanating from the environment that people now create and discover. As the regional economy is transformed to better fit into the international division of labour, its components are similarly transformed. This includes all aspects of the environment, such as housing, as well as that remnant of what is generally called the 'natural' environment. However, it must be argued that nature is continuously produced and reproduced in forms and patterns reflective of the processes of a particular mode of production. Consequently, devalorised landscape, a landscape of slums and decline.

A further consequence of capitalist development is the increased risk and hazardous exposure to the population, particularly the most vulnerable segments. Greater vulnerability is generated in a system dominated by the drive to accumulate capital in a class society. Because of the incessant attempt to transform the environment into exchange-values, and to treat its unproductive aspects as 'externalities', the firm, in the throes of the anarchy of production, does not internalise the costs of control except when under mandate from government. Environmental pollution is a symptom of an alienation affecting the entire society, separating it from commodified nature and placing despoiled nature in opposition to the population.

Thus, it is no surprise that working class housing is often found on the downwind side of industrial areas. It is also clear that, in the face of devalorisation, it is the working class and especially, the reserve army of the unemployed who are most vulnerable because they have been and are being integrated into fuller commodity relations to the exclusion of other forms of social survival. The individual is isolated and alienated and subjected to rapid erosion of the ability to maintain particular standards of life quality. This vulnerability is reflected, for example, in Brenner's conclusions concerning 37,000 additional deaths predicted on the basis of recent increases in the unemployment rate in the United States. 13. This is also suggested by the greater rate of increase in cancer among black males, more marginal members of the U.S. economy, than white males as industrial employment increased. 14.

The Northern Region of England

Devalorisation induced transformation of a regional economic structure and the labour force should be evident in a specific regional context. Two aspects of devalorisation are examined below. One focuses upon the economics of capital production and social reproduction, while the other discusses associated spatial change in the regional economy. The northern region of England provides such a case.

Dependent upon four heavy industries for the balance of this century, the Northern region is particularly susceptible to cyclical downturns or crises. The Northern region has suffered through seven economic crises between 1945 and 1971 with three occurring between 1961 and 1971. 15. The

severity of these crises was much greater, as
measured by employment impact, in the Northern
region relative to Great Britain. During this period
the region experienced substantial structural transformation with more rapid change occurring during
the 1961 to 1971 decade as would be expected due to
the incidence of three crises. Change in the region
is characterised by growth in the service sector,
increased diversification of manufacturing industries to include more consumer goods production, and
less reliance upon the traditional heavy industries
of the region.

During the 1960s, the degree of extra-regional
control over plants and firms in the Northern region
grew significantly. With the exception of the four
traditional heavy industries, the 'other' manufacturing industries have increasingly become branches
or subsidiaries of firms headquartered outside the
region. In the early 1960s, about 50 percent of the
'other' manufacturing firms in the Northern region
were branch plants or subsidiaries of extra-regional
firms. Between 1962 and 1973 the number jumped 152
percent, accounting for an increase in total
manufacturing employment in the region from 58 to 77
percent in subsidiaries and branches. By 1973, 70
percent of the 'other' manufacturing firms were
branches or subsidiaries of extra-regional firms.

Between 1962 and 1973, the number of regionally
owned plants decreased, while the non-regional subsidiaries and branches increased considerably, as
would be expected in a devalorisation explanation of
regional change. Transnational corporations consti-
tuted a significant percent of new firms in the
region. Of 260 maufacturing firms entering the
Northern region between 1963 and 1971, 43.5 percent
were subsidiaries or branches of transnational
corporations, providing 55.6 percent of new manufacturing employment in the region. 16. Almost a third
of the TNC associated firms that have entered the
region since 1963 are U.S. based and account for 18
percent of all new manufacturing employment.

In the Northern region, the expectations of the
devalorisation explanation are further fulfilled in
the changing profile of the labour force. New industry to the region is the dynamic growth cluster for
employment. The rate of employment increase was
greater in new industries than in the indigenous
industries, and their share of regional employment
increased threefold from 4.7 percent in 1952 to 14.0
percent in 1973. During the 1963-1973 decade, in the
course of three economic crises, the rate of growth

for the new industries was the highest yet, while
the indigenous industries evidenced employment
decreases.

Furthermore, the labour market reflected a
shift from primary to secondary labour. 17. Since
World War II, women have become more active in the
labour force. In Great Britain, there was an
increase of 10.61 percent in the total work force
from 1952 to 1973. During the same period, employment for women increased by more than twice the
average, at 28.08 percent. In the Northern region,
the total increase in employment was 4.64 percent.
Again, female employment increased by 38.59 percent
while there was a decrease in male employment of
9.09 percent.

During the decade of the 1960s, new firms and
industrial diversification provided the greatest
source of female employment in the Northern region.
However, because the single largest source of new
female employment was in low level clerical jobs in
the service sector, and due to lower wages for such
employment and for females relative to males, this
has resulted in reduced personal income in the
area. 18. In the Northern region, in manufacturing
and service industries, men received 58 percent more
than women for manual employment and 60 percent more
for non-manual employment (April 1977).

Personal disposable income in the Northern
region was 11.6 percent lower than the United
Kingdom average in 1971, and actual personal income
per person in the North was consistently 15 percent
below the U.K. between 1961 and 1971. It is only
through progressive taxation and high social
security payments that the difference has been
reduced to 12 percent.

Spatial Changes

The full complexity of changes in the spatial
organisation of a regional economy undergoing
capital restructuring and an associated industrial
structural transformation would require an entire
exposition in itself. However, a brief discussion of
a few of the associated changes, promoted by state
devalorised capital investment, are indicative of
the impacts of the overall process.

In the Northern region, spatial polarisation is
becoming more extreme due, in part, to the New Towns
policies. Created as growth centres, and located in
the eastern portion of the region, these new towns
have absorbed manufacturing firms immigrating to the

region so that they account for 20 percent of new employment. While employment in the region as a whole has decreased by 3 percent, employment in the new towns increased by 34 percent from 1969-1973. Furthermore, 87 percent of the firms locating in the new towns are subsidiaries and branches of extra-regional firms, the ones most likely to export capital from the region and to respond to decisions taken in the interest of the total corporation by the headquarters firms outside the region. 19.

As mentioned above, the other aspect of the polarisation process is the changing population settlement pattern in the region which has the effect of providing the new towns with a labour force. This has been promoted, in part, by government housing policies directing new housing construction to the new towns. Thus, in one county, Tyne and Wear, 80 percent of the net increase in public sector housing was in three new towns between 1971 and 1975. The impact of new housing location combined with effective 'red lining' of entire areas within a region (promoting devalorisation of capital stock), such as occurred in Northwest Durham, is to cause a major restructuring and reorientation of the regional population's life activity patterns. 20. Changes wrought by capital restructuring may wreak havoc upon patterns of social production and repro-duction that have historically evolved.

The changes in the structure and patterns of the Northern region of England support the devalorisation explanation of industrial structural transformation. During three economic crises in the 1960s, when the rate of capital accumulation declined, local smaller 'capitals' diminished in regional importance while branches and subsidiaries of extra-regional firms increased to account for 70 percent of non-traditional manufacturing enterprises in the region. Increasing centralisation and concentration of capital is further highlighted by the number of TNCs, accounting for at least 43.5 percent of new firms in the region and 55.6 percent of new manufacturing employment in the 1960s. Associated changes in the labour force also support the devalorisation explan-ation. As female labour increased by 38.6 percent and male labour decreased by 10.0 percent, personal disposable income remained below the U.K. average, due, in part, to lower wages in the new firms. Able to reduce costs and labour-relations difficulties by changing industrial technologies, TNCs are in a position to attain suitable rates of return in the Northern region, as in other places where they have

come to be significant economic actors. In addition,
government policies and investment patterns contributed to the spatial reorientation of the Northern
region. Industrial estates, new towns policies, and
provision of public housing all promoted spatial
polarisation within the region. In the Northern
region, the eastern portion contains the growth
areas, while the western section of the region has
been systematically devalorised without immediate
prospects of new investment and revalorisation.

Conclusion
By approaching the phenomenon of regional economic
transformation from the perspective of political
economy, the capitalist system is treated as a
changing complex of international production and
social relations. Driven by the need to accumulate
capital, there has been a historical development of
the international division of labour promoted by
historically pre-eminent forms of international
enterprise. For the most part, since World War II,
TNCs have maintained global economic dominance as a
function of centralised capital control and the
ability to rapidly change investment priorities in
line with sectoral and spatial changes in profit
rates.
     Contradictory forces are released in the drive
to accumulate capital that may engender profit rate
decline instead of increase. An extreme case arises
when transnational corporations achieve such control
in a sector as to become almost synonymous with it.
Necessarily, the logic of the system dictates
sectoral devalorisation in order to preserve capital
value and restore conditions of future profitability.
For host regions and declining sectors, the consequences may be devastating. Devalorisation leads to
a capital restructuring process in which the entire
regional political economy is affected, ranging from
production relations, including types of employment
and wage levels, to changes in social reproduction
accompanying reorganisation of the spatial landscape.

FOOTNOTES

1. Paul M. Sweezy, <u>The Theory of Capitalist Development</u> (New York, Monthly Review Press, 1942), p.80; Folker Frobel, et al, "The Tendency Towards A New International Division of Labour", <u>Review</u>, 1,1 (Summer 1977), 73; David Harvey, "The Geography of Capitalist Accumulation", <u>Antipode</u> 7,2 (September 1975), 9.
2. David Harvey, "The Geography of Capitalist Accumulation", <u>Antipode</u> 7,2 (September 1975), 10.
3. Joseph M. Gillman, <u>The Falling Rate of Profit: Marx's Law and Its Significance to Twentieth Century Capitalism</u> (London, Dennis Dobson, 1957), p.1.
4. The rate of profit is represented as $P = S'(1-q)$ where:

P = rate of profit
S'= rate of surplus-value which also equals the surplus-value (s)/variable capital (v)
q = organic composition of capital which also equals constant capital (c)/ variable capital (v)

and where: surplus-value (s) represents value created by labour-power in excess of the value of the wage bill (variable capital component). For the full derivation of these relationships, see Sweezy, op. cit., pp. 56-71.
5. United States Congress, Senate Commission on Finance, <u>The Multinational Corporation and the World Economy</u> (Washington, U.S. Government Printing Office, February 26, 1973), pp. 2-3.
6. Transfer pricing is discussed by William Dymza, <u>Multinational Business Strategy</u>, (New York, McGraw-Hill Book Company, 1972), p. 158. Double accounting is discussed by Michael Z. Brooke and H. Lee Remmers, <u>The Multinational Corporation in Europe - Some Key Problems</u> (Ann Arbor, The University of Michigan Press, 1972), p. 18. International financial sources including Eurobond markets are discussed in Robert Z. Aliber, <u>The International Money Game</u> (New York, Basic Books, Inc., 1973); Bob Edwards, <u>Multinational Companies and the Trade Unions</u> (Nottingham, Russell Press Ltd., 1977); Brian Tew, <u>The Evolution of the International Monetary System</u> 1945-1977 (New York, John Wiley & Sons, 1977).

7.   Geza P. Lauter and Paul M. Dickie, <u>Multi-national Corporations and East European Socialist Economies</u> (New York, Praeger Publishers, 1975).

8.   This discussion is placed within a context of value rates of profit rather than price rates of profit. A discussion of the devalorisation concept may be found in C.G. Pickvance, "Housing, Reproduction of Capital and Reproduction of Labour-Power: Some Recent French Works", <u>Antipode</u> 8,11 (1976), pp. 58-68.

9.   Katherine Gibson, Julie Graham, and Don Shakow, "Labour Market Phenomena and the Falling Rate of Profit: A Theoretical Prospectus", Clark University Regional Development Unit Working Paper (March 1979).

10. S.J. Prais, <u>The Evolution of Giant Firms in Britain - A Study of the Growth of Concentration in Manufacturing Industry in Britain 1909-1970</u> (Cambridge, Cambridge University Press, 1976), p.124.

11. For discussion of productive and non-productive state expenditure, see: Paul Kattick, <u>Marx and Keynes - The Limits of the Mixed Economy</u> (Boston, Extending Horizon Books, 1969), p. 117; James Becker, <u>Marxian Political Economy</u> (New York, Cambridge University Press, 1977), p. 191; Karl Marx, <u>Capital</u>, Volume II (New York, International Publishers, 1967), p. 136; Claus Offe, "The Abolition of Market Control and the Problem of Legitimacy (I) and (II)", <u>Kapitalistate</u>, nos. 1 and 2, 1973.

12. For example, in the United Kingdom, while the share in profits in net output in private industry averaged 19.7 percent between 1950 and 1970, it was only 4.9 percent in public corporations.

13. Ben Bedell, "Jobless Suffer Plethora of Woes", <u>The Guardian</u>, June 18, 1980, p. 7.

14. Robert C. Harriss, Christoph Hohenemser and Robert W. Kates, "Our Hazardous Environment", <u>Environment</u> 20, 7 (September 1978), p. 13.

15. S. Menshikov, <u>The Economic Cycle: Post-War Developments</u> (Moscow, Progress Publishers, 1977), p. 45.

16. Documentation of transnational corporate activity in the Northern region was accomplished by use of the Employment Data Bank of Newcastle University in conjunction with Community Development Project, Multinationals in Tyne and Wear (Newcastle, Community Development Project, 1977) and North of England Development Council, <u>International Investment in the Northern Region</u> (Newcastle 1977).

17. Primary labour refers to highly paid, organised and highly skilled, usually male workers

with relative job stability. Secondary labour is
precisely the opposite. See Thomas Vietorisz and
Bennett Harrison, "Labour Market Segmentation:
Positive Feedback and Divergent Development", Papers
and Proceedings of the American Economic Association
(May 1973), pp. 366-376.

18. Northern Region Strategy Team (NRST),
Technical Report No. 4, Growth and Structural Change
in the Economy of the Northern Region Since 1952
(Newcastle, NRST, January 1976), p. 50.

19. NRST, Technical Report No. 4, op.cit., p.23.

20. Durham Planning Committee, "Minutes",
October 18, 1950, p. 5; January 23, 1971, p. 3.

GLOBAL CAPITALISM AND REGIONAL DECLINE: IMPLICATIONS FOR THE STRATEGY OF CLASSES IN OLDER REGIONS

Robert Ross
Katherine Gibson
Julie Graham
Philip O'Keefe
Don M. Shakow
Paul Susman

GLOBAL CAPITALISM AND REGIONAL DECLINE: IMPLICATIONS FOR THE STRATEGY OF CLASSES IN OLDER REGIONS

Introduction

Job loss and plant closings, and the consequent deterioration of conditions of life, have been discussed in reference to the U.S. Northeast and Midwest. In turn, the somewhat more vigorous economies of other U.S. regions are contrasted to these mature ones. Recently, Marxist analysts and others have attended to the international context of these North American phenomena. They note two critical accompaniments of regional decline. First, the flow of capital away from the venerable regions of industrial concentration has a major international component. Capital is not merely being transferred to the U.S. Sunbelt; increasingly, Third World and backward European sites have been chosen by U.S. investors as locations for new productive facilities. Second, the transnational conglomerate (TNC) is the characteristic agent of such capital allocations.

In addition to these observations, however, others are required to properly orient theoretical work and political strategy in the coming period:

First, the experience of the U.S. Northeast and Midwest is by no means unique among the advanced capitalist countries. The North of England - e.g. County Durham, Tyne and Wear - and South Wales in the U.K., the Lorraine steel-working and Pas de Calais regions in France, and Wallonia in Belgium all similarly experience decisions made by the purveyors of large scale capital, to avoid or withdraw from the mature industrial areas of the capitalist world.

Second, the resultant flows of capital to areas of manufacturing growth appear to be compelled by a new and vigorous level of competition among TNCs of varying national origin. This competition forces

each enterprise to use its global information
resources, economic leverage, and political influence to seek out sites for productive investment
which minimise labour costs and working class
militance.

In addition to these observations, it is
important to understand that the metaphoric use of
the notion 'decline', while fruitful, must be
supplemented by a conception of structural change in
the older regions. The 'restructuring' of regional
economies has two aspects, variously observed in
different regions. In regard to the labour process,
the new global system enables the employer to dis-
aggregate the production process over space. Here,
research, development and administration; there,
skilled machining and fabrication; still elsewhere,
semi-skilled assembly. Everywhere, or wherever
possible, in new production processes, investors
attempt to liberate capital from dependence on
particular groups or skills among labour, and to
design these human capacities into the machine.
Restructuring as evidenced in the changing relations
of capital to labour is facilitated by parallel
changes in the organisation and structure of
capital. In the older regions, visible shifts to a
new industrial base are often the outward signs of
changes in the corporate structure of capital. Consider, for example, the increasing prominence of
conglomerate firms which are multisectoral as well
as multinational in scope. Such firms are not only
relatively footloose in space, but almost entirely
flexible in their orientation to particular product
and service lines. Their presence in a region signals
labour's vulnerability to capitalist class decision
makers with an expanding range of investment options.

The manifold social and political consequences
of structural change merit attention but are only
partially and imperfectly reflected in current
theories of, for example, the world system or the
internationalisation of capital. This presentation
focuses on the changing strategic balance of power
in the older regions and locates the origins of
these changes in the larger theoretical and strategic
context of the emergence of a global capitalism.

The emerging international division of labour,
and the global scope of capital flows, imply that
capital has adopted the use of spatial and sectoral
mobility as a major instrument in its struggle with
labour. It is in this process and this changed
terrain of struggle that one should locate the
origins of the ostensibly conservative political

climate, in the U.S. and elsewhere, for the changed
terms of class contest represent palpable advantages
for capital.

This may be illustrated in a small case from
Worcester, Massachusetts. The Johnson Wire Corporation employs approximately 300 skilled and semi-
skilled steelworkers there. In recent contract
negotiations the employer held fast to an extremely
poor offer to the union. It attempted to enforce its
demands on labour with the <u>threat</u> to move production
to an existing Mississippi plant with equivalent
technical capacity and a much lower wage structure.
The Worcester workers were faced with a cruel choice
of accepting a lower standard of living or perhaps
losing their jobs.

The example of Johnson Wire is but one of
thousands. The threat to move to a low wage, non-
union region within a nation is, with increasing
frequency, a threat to move to another nation with
even lower wages. The conflict between capital and
labour is now acted out on a world scale.

Global Capitalism
Under global capitalism, historic tendencies such as
automation and deskilling are no less evident, but
the potential number of production locations expands
dramatically. When a new technology becomes available, or a given sector expands, the investor has
the ability to decide where to locate facilities: in
an already established locale, or in some other.
Needless to say, regional sentiment or concern for
local communities is not evident in such calculations, but the costs of labour, its degree of organisation and consciousness, and the local political
situation are. Thus manufacturing investment in the
last decade or so has flowed increasingly to low
wage and poorly or unorganised labour environments.
In the American South, the Caribbean, and the
Pacific Rim, new technologies may be introduced
without struggle over the prerogatives of management, and at extremely low wage rates. Liberated
from an exclusive orientation to particular regions,
capitalists may place routine assembly facilities at
such low wage sites even while they maintain headquarters and R and D functions in labour markets
with advanced capitalist urban standards of living.
Such latter areas may experience erosion of their
industrial base, and concomitant expansion of non-
productive activities such as office and distribution work.

Effectively, the workers of the mature urban industrial areas are now joined by workers of the Third World in the same global reserve of industrial labour. This alters the conditions of class struggle generally. It erodes the workers' level and quality of life directly, through an altered labour-capital relation. And it also changes the relation of political forces in cities and regions, further worsening the situation of workers in the sphere of reproduction.

National and local government - the state - mediates and abets many of the impacts of this transformation. Class responses to what is experienced as local or regional decline, in both its production and consumption aspects, have often involved demands directed at state policy and institutions. These demands are formed within two kinds of structural constraints: the nature of the state under capitalism; and the relation of the state both to economic space and to the social terrain created by the specific, often local, history of capital and labour's struggle.

The State

The state is an institution with a monopoly of legitimate violence. In class societies, it ensures the continued domination of one class over others. This domination may take many forms. Only rarely does class domination through the state rely exclusively on coercion. Rather, such domination usually consists of sufficient force to resist outright challenges and, as well, subtle and diffuse bonds of apparently voluntary loyalty. Thus, to secure their continuing domination, to reproduce the class system, capitalists must have hegemony in the sphere of ideology. Ideological reproduction of capitalism is carried out in many institutions - the churches, the family, the schools, the mass media - but the ultimate responsibility for ideological reproduction rests primarily with the state. Let us call this responsibility, as O'Connor does, the necessary task of legitimation. 1.

The legitimation function has two aspects: the first is the legitimation of the system of capitalism as a whole. 'Free enterprise', 'legitimate profits', 'equality before the law', and the 'right to make peaceful change' - these are some of the symbolic assurances by which officials of the state and other ideological media communicate to the population that they live under the best of all

possible arrangements. It is typical of such formulations that they are overlaid with heavy doses of
national chauvinism, that is, they refer to the
ineffable value of the 'American' or 'British' way
of life. This leads us to the second aspect of
legitimation.

The state itself must appear to be a community
of the whole people, and an instrument of the aggregated will of the majority. Most decidedly it must
not appear to be the exclusive instrument of one
class. In North America, Western Europe and elsewhere, parliamentary democracy has become the
institutional and ideological expression of this
form of legitimation. If state policies are less
than efficacious, or less than equitable, responsibility for these deficiencies is placed at the door-
step of the presumably equal citizens.

Legitimating itself and the system is a critical task of the state at both national and local
levels. This is a difficult enterprise, for the
state has other essential tasks. There are varied
and massive requirements entailed in extracting and
accumulating surplus value for which the state has
been historically responsible and increasingly
necessary. The vast physical infrastructure of
modern life - roads, water supplies, physical
security from fire and brigandage - all require
state provision. In these functions, the state
socialises many of the costs of production, while
ensuring the juridicial right of capital to appropriate privately the profits derived from production. The state is responsible for much more than
these social overhead costs: it acts as a source of
investment capital in a variety of ways which may be
termed subsidies. These range from tax expenditures
to outright extensions of public capital to private
owners.

Many aspects of state policy are difficult to
categorise as serving the purposes of either legitimation or accumulation, for they serve both functions. Welfare payments, for example, operate to
diffuse and co-opt potential militance, thereby
providing a legitimating social peace; but they also
physically sustain surplus labourers who remain
available as reserves of low wage labour, and whose
(even) minimal purchasing power supports aggregate
demand for commodities.

At any given moment and, as we shall see
shortly, in any given place, the tasks of legitimation and accumulation may come into more or less
direct conflict. When austerity programmes cause

neighbourhoods to lose state monies, say, for social services to children, in order that a city may offer downtown developers a more fashionable mall or plaza for executive offices, citizens may perceive the imperatives of accumulation as odious. When energy producers demand higher profits for dubious invest- ments, citizens may question the neutrality of state intervention. When state or federal courts enjoin a strike, workers may wonder whose side the law is on. One of the key legitimating strategies of the sixties was the expansion of municipal payrolls, the hiring of many thousands of persons, black, white and brown, who otherwise would have been poor and would have been potential participants in insurgent move- ments. This was the larger though less well publici- sed of the poverty programmes; and, from the point of view of capital, and the resident bourgeoisie of the cities, it had the consequence of creating a municipal tax hunger beyond the conventional means of municipal revenue sources. Now, regions experien- cing capital out-flow are pressed by both these forces to adopt austerity budgets, releasing employees, and to extend wider and deeper subsidies to investors.

We see then that the state has necessary legitimation and accumulation tasks and these may be in contradiction. Let us turn to the historical property of social space.

The Social Terrain
Economic and social life have spatial dimensions. Any given place, a unit of governmental jurisdiction or a market area, has a history of development - social, economic and political. Rapid economic development or change concentrated in a given area brings new people and new social - that is, ethnic, racial or class - groups to it. Between 1880-1920, for example, the U.S. saw millions of Southern and Eastern European peoples brought to the industrial- ising urban concentrations of the nation. Employers used these flows of migrants as a more or less conscious means to undermine emerging working class solidarity. In the South Chicago Steel Works of U.S. Steel, for example, foremen were instructed to tell Italians that their English co-workers would desert them in strike action. 2.

Over time, the resident working class may find means of overcoming its divisions, of moulding itself as a class. It may (and it has in the U.S. Northeast) use in its interest the liberties which legitimate the democratic state. It may and it has formed unions and other associations of class interest for class conflict purposes. Since the state must, to some minimal degree, continue to legitimate itself as more than the instrument of capitalists, this process may result in certain accomplishments: the abolition of child labour; the achievement of workers' compensation, unemployment compensation, social security, welfare, housing subsidies, and so forth. True, some of these policies may prove to be in capital's larger interest - but not necessarily because all capitalists realise it, and not necessarily in the interests of all capitalists.

Over time, then, a place develops a particular social and political configuration, a characteristic terrain. The Massachusetts legal and social terrain - unemployment compensation, for example, and welfare payments - show the local working class to have been relatively successful as compared to others. In general, this can be said of the entire Northeast industrial belt of the U.S. Rates of unionisation are higher, and many aspects of the social wage are also higher than, for example, in the Southern U.S. 3. To give one qualitative illustration, until 1975 Massachusetts workers could collect unemployment compensation while on strike. A 'liberal' governor, under pressure from business and financial groups during a grave recession, introduced the legislation which took this right away.

Thus, a nation and, indeed, the world is a mosaic not only of technical and economic dimensions, but a differentiated juridical terrain in which capital and labour have had varying degrees of relative success. This terrain is the result of the tensions produced in part by the legitimation-accumulation dialectic.

But even modest local success by workers has been achieved within the larger context of dominant capitalism. The fact that capital is more mobile than labour, and that capital is structurally dominant in the system at large, means that local gains made by workers which are not nationally or internationally uniform, may produce capital mobility to a more propitious social and political terrain, and/or the threat of such mobility as a means of disciplining local labour, forcing it to relinquish past or future advantages.

In light of these considerations, let us examine the strategic initiatives of capital and labour in the older regions of the United States.

Capitalist Class Strategic Initiatives

In North America, the local state is the focus of political activity for the locally based business class. Those businesses which depend specifically on regional markets and land use patterns are those whose representatives are most likely to become activists. Commercial and real estate interests, locally based banks, newspaper and other media interests are examples 4., as is the scatter of small competitive sector manufacturing firms. In the face of local transformation, such interests, often with the support of local labour (especially in the building trades), turn to state institutions and to translocal capital for assistance in maintaining the viability of their enterprises. Local capital creates coalitions oriented to changing the priorities of the local state towards direct and enlarged outlays for infrastructure and for subsidies to potential investors. With such inducements in hand, local business leaders and public officials approach the controllers of large scale investments, attempting to attract economic activity to their jurisdictions and market areas.

In a previous paper, we have analysed such strategies as having two modes: the competitive mode, which seeks to attract the remaining manufacturing potential of a region to a given jurisdiction; and the structural mode, which seeks to abet the transformation of urban economies toward characteristic retail and service sector agglomerations. 5. Both of these strategic modes require the local state to subsidise immigrant capital through a variety of tax, capital provision, and infrastructural schemes. Both require that the local state transform the political terrain in ways which will be perceived by potential investors as creating a propitious environment for new economic activity.

Consumer and labour activists call the demands for this environment the 'business climate' argument in relation to working class demands on the state. It amounts to attempts to drive down the social wage.

The credible threat to leave a region or to curtail investments enforces capital's programme. The relative tax burden on the salaries of executives and professional/technical workers, for example, is seen by the directors of the new electronics and information processing firms in Massachusetts as a barrier to successful recruitment of such persons in a national labour market. They thus persist in a campaign for the restriction of state taxation, and therefore for restriction of state expenditures on those functions they do not value. Social services, and redistributive expenditure programmes in general, come under steady attack. Their explicit agreement with the conservative governor of the state is that they will continue to expand employment in the state only if state taxation decreases.

Financial institutions play significant roles in the changing balance of power. Holding large amounts of local government debt, the larger regional banks can choose to exert decisive pressure on public budgets by refusing to extend further credit when the fiscal capacities of local units of government appear to be imprudently extended. The role of New York City financial institutions during that city's fiscal crisis of 1975-78 is typical. In return for continued credit, New York City has given legal veto power over its budget to an agency explicitly representative of the financial interests holding New York paper - the Emergency Financial Control Board.

The strategic agenda of capitalist class political activists in response to the new situation is quite comprehensive. As employers they seek to resist wage and benefit demands by threatening to relocate if labour is recalcitrant. As political actors, they resist and/or attempt to rescind those burdensome policies which protect the quality of life of workers and other residents through, for example, environmental or occupational health and safety regulations. Among the early casualities of the re-structuring of regional capital is the loosening of air pollution regulations. In another example, we note that in Massachusetts, the High Technology Council (a private industry group close to the current governor) has been successful in provoking the restructuring of public secondary and higher education, inducing plans to focus on their needs for personnel familiar with or prepared to learn the various tasks necessary to the computer and electronics industry. As the single growing manufacturing sector in the state, their political influence is rivalled only by that of financial institutions.

Such political initiatives have been broadly successful. Everywhere in the older regions, benefits and programmes obtained through the last twenty years of consumer and labour activity are being withdrawn as attention is focused on the desperate 'need' to court investment by a business class which has a more or less clear set of prerequisites. Such political successes evidence the political ability

of both translocal and local investors to convince
labour that such transformations are both necessary
and helpful in maintaining jobs and levels of
living. This persuasion is implemented by mass media
which accept the arguments at face value, and by
politicians who act as the carriers of bad news
which necessarily requires austerity.

These ideological definitions of the situation
are not unopposed, nor are they perfectly efficacious. As we showed in our work on local development
strategies, capital's ability to effect local
political change is greater than its willingness to
invest in older regions. And, however late, labour
acting in its interests both as producer of value
and as consumer of commodities and services has
begun to develop discernible responses. To date, the
responses to restructuring of capital and labour,
and decline in the sphere of reproduction, have been
primarily, though not exclusively, defensive.

Working Class Strategic Response

Organising in the Sphere of Production

The main vehicle by which workers attempt to defend
their interests is the labour union. The shift of
manufacturing away from highly unionised environments has weakened the unions politically, and has
eroded their membership base, which is falling as a
proportion of the labour force. Nevertheless, unions
attempt to hold onto the wage and benefit packages
they have won, and to include in collective bargaining agreements some protection against structural
shift. The more powerful monopoly sector industrial
unions (for example, auto, rubber, and steel
workers) attempt to obtain contract provisions which
ensure notification in advance of lay-offs or shut-
downs, and which provide severance pay linked to the
years of service of employees.

These efforts are not spectacularly successful.
The real wages of American workers are no higher now
than they were ten years ago, and have declined in
the last five years; and only 30-34 percent of the
major collective bargaining agreements include the
notification and severance payment provisions. This
means that less than 10 percent of American workers
are covered by such agreements.

In the political sphere, labour's primary
responses have been traditional protectionism and
also more progressive proposals which either hinder
the spatial mobility of capital or seek indemnifica-

tion for it. For example, the United Auto Workers
(UAW) supports, in the federal legislature and in a
number of the industrial state legislatures,
policies which would make notification and severance
benefits a matter of law covering all relocations,
not just those covered by collective bargaining
agreements. The UAW and other unions also propose
the abolition of features of the U.S. tax code which
give investors financial incentives to close older
installations and to physically relocate. Similarly,
a number of unions support abolition of tax code
provisions which treat favourably the foreign earnings of TNCs. 6. These policies, one should note,
can be evaluated for their efficacy through an
analysis of the experience of the Federal Republic
of Germany, Sweden and the United Kingdom which have
rather more rigorous legal restrictions on relocations. 7.

In any case, these are strategically defensive,
reactive responses. To the extent that the need for
reinvestment is perceived, current proposals look to
federal revenues as subsidies to private investors
in older areas, rather than proposing labour or
state controlled enterprises as such. Some discussion
has been devoted to state policy which would facilitate worker acquisition of threatened plants, but
thus far experiments with such schemes have not been
compelling, for the installations turned into
co-operatives, etc., have in most cases been marginal and technically obsolescent.

Organising in the Sphere of Consumption
In their roles as consumers and citizens, workers
have responded to the deterioration of community
institutions and services somewhat more militantly
and exuberantly, but still defensively. In the older
regions of the U.S., urban populist organisations
have flourished in the last five to ten years. These
social movement organisations are independent of the
political parties and are composed of employed working class and petty bourgeois city residents. They
tend to focus on consumption and public service
issues such as local taxes, utility rates, arson,
and bank 'redlining' (the refusal to extend housing
mortgage credit in a given area). In short, they are
quite similar, if not identical, to those groups
Castells has characterised as "urban social movements". 8. The similarity in composition and focus
suggests that their strategic situations may also be
quite similar. If that is the case, then our

analysis leaves us less sanguine than Castells about their potential for success. Though we share his appreciation of the energy and aspirations of such groups, we would tend to emphasise the strategic limits they encounter.

The language of the populist groups expresses their political situation. Although some of the organisers are people with socialist ideas, the constituency shares the anti-socialist ideology of hegemonic capitalism. Thus, the political rhetoric of these groups is that of 'economic democracy', pitting the grassroots against corporate power. It calls vaguely for a redistribution of wealth and power. It condemns the callous disregard for community and human welfare evidenced by the conglomerates which remove capital from the cities and older regions while calling for subsidies. At best, this movement is suffused with populist militance which borders on class awareness.

In assessing the limits of populist groups in the present political and strategic context, the limits of a local focus, and the related limits of a focus on the sphere of consumption are particularly worthy of attention. The following analysis deals with each of these in turn.

A typical form of the populist movement organisation is a basis in neighbourhood chapters. Members become involved in issues which are quite local and immediate: abandoned buildings, traffic problems, etc. Chapters, once stabilised, will participate in city-wide campaigns. In Worcester, Massachusetts, for example, a chapter of a prominent neighbourhood-based populist organisation recently campaigned to expose large developers and landlords who were tax delinquents. At a state-wide level, utility rates, taxes and, recently, the plant closing notification legislation discussed earlier have been the subject of campaigns.

The problem in the longer run is that even hard fought victories in such matters affect but a small part of the overall deterioration which is generated and controlled at more distant levels of power and authority. Locality organising always faces the fact that at bottom capital resources are not allocated on the basis of purely local considerations.

At the present conjuncture, local reform is made both more difficult and more dangerous by the expanding context in which important business decisions are made. Each municipal or state/provincial reform is met with the threat of capital mobility. Some of these threats are merely attempts

to discourage local activism and citizen demands.
But some of them are quite real. As we have seen,
long-standing features of the local terrain are
compared by investors to the qualities of other and
distant terrains. Even within the national arena of
the U.S., the fact that there are 50 state legislative arenas creates the potential for continual
variation in local configurations of capital-labour
relations. Thus, an advance for workers in one
state, if not matched elsewhere within a relevant
time period, may be the occasion for capital withdrawal from the progressive state and relocation to
a more retrograde domain. This will bolster the
austerity atmosphere in the former locality, stiffen
the opposition to local working class demands, and
in general act to suppress the possibility of local
success.

In summary, the local base and focus of the new
populism is constrained by the disproportionality
between the needs and problems of constituents and
the power and resources available at the local level;
by the centrifugal tendency of the many local
groups, which makes national action difficult; and
by the ability of capital to obviate or forestall
local gains by moving or threatening to move to more
propitious locations.

The limitations of localism are related to and
highlighted by the limitations on organising residents in their roles as consumers. Central city
neighbourhoods are infrequently populated by people
with the same employer or even in the same industry.
When they are, as, for example, in certain Chicago
steelworkers' neighbourhoods, community activity,
union activism, and local politics may converge in a
fashion which facilitates class awareness. 9. More
typically, however, neighbourhoods are diverse
occupationally though homogeneous in income and
ethnic terms. The typical job structures of modern
enterprise create a diversity of occupational niches
which often obscure the underlying and common class
situation of the employees. Furthermore, the social
and political history of American labour unions has
produced a relatively narrow orientation to the job
as distinct from the community interests of union
members. This has generated political isolation, for
there is also a certain distrust - insularity, if
you will - in the attitude of local and regional
union officials toward social activists who are
based outside the official labour movement. In consequence, workers' neighbourhood problems are not
usually perceived as 'workers' issues; rather, they

are viewed through the ideological screen of the
citizen role.

In this role, the aggrieved citizen demands
equity from government, and resists business class
demands that make the task of maintaining a house-
hold more arduous. Thus, it is the populist movement
rather than the labour movement that organises and
channels the anger and activism provoked by the
deterioration of economic and environmental conditions in the neighbourhoods of declining cities and
regions.

We have already suggested the inherent limits
of local action on such matters, and similar limits
constrain action in the sphere of consumption,
collective or individual. For example, by the time
the withdrawal of bank loans for housing becomes a
visible public issue in an area, one has moved quite
far along in the chain of resource allocation.
Financial institutions have decided on regional
locations toward or away from which they will direct
their investments; they have also decided on a mix
of housing and other forms of investment, and a mix
of long and short term loans for the next period.
These decisions have been heavily constrained by
national monetary policy. In turn, this policy is
dictated by calculations at the level of international finance - for example, the relation of the
dollar to other competitor currencies. At this
highly aggregated level, investment flows are determined by changes in labour's position vis-a-vis
capital in a vast number of local sites. Thus, the
consumer of housing credit is at the end of a very
long queue of decisions; and the decision-makers at
whom the point-of-consumption organisers direct
their demands have little left to distribute and
little discretion in its distribution.

This is ever the dilemma of populist strategies.
By focusing on local, area-defined worker and
consumer interests, a populist organisation is able
to develop a popular base even though, or because,
it avoids socialist rhetoric. But by so organising
workers, it operates where their action is less
efficacious than when they can organise against
their employers in struggle over the value they
produce.

Initiatives Toward Unification

Under the regime of monopoly capital, workers in
monopoly industries had more power when organised in
relation to employers than they could obtain through

the more diffuse structures of neighbourhood action.
Currently that power is being eroded by the global
deployment of capital, and the social and local
consequences of this process are extremely distress-
ful. An obvious strategic response is the joining of
labour and community groups or, more importantly,
the forging of class unity around these various
issues understood in class terms.

The new populists do perceive this as a desirable project. In Massachusetts, Connecticut and
Ohio, for example, labour-citizen action coalitions
have formed to support the plant closing legislation
mentioned earlier. Though basically defensive, the
plant closing coalitions merit examination for other
reasons. They begin the extremely difficult process
of uniting the interest groups and therefore the
interests of workers in their separated roles as
producers and consumers. The process of argument and
coalition formation which is entailed in such legislative struggles creates, to varying degrees, challenges to business hegemony over the context of
political discourse. That capital does not have the
right to destroy communities, unmindful of costs;
that workers and citizens do have the right to constrain capital mobility - these principles are
required for forging class unity and eroding the
legitimacy of business dominance.

The activists in these coalitions accurately
state that the current 'business climate' argument
gives local capitalist activists a great deal of
leverage in curtailing or defeating programmes
supported by citizens and labour groups. The plant
closing controversy inevitably opens such arguments
to scrutiny. It may become a matter of general knowledge, for instance, that a large proportion of
closings and job losses are effected by conglomerates and TNCs whose decisions may not reflect an
estimation of a subsidiary's viability so much as a
particular tax advantage or the high target rate it
sets for acceptable profits. Coalition activists
report that the focus on conglomerates makes it
easier to oppose 'business climate' arguments, for
the conglomerates are readily portrayed as manipulative and not to be trusted. Finally, the activists
claim that though national legislation is desirable,
local movements and victories will hasten it. In
other words, the organisers of these campaigns value
the benefits such legislation would give workers,
but they value at least as much the political implications of forming and winning them. They point the
way to a more conscious and unified class politics.

Structural Constraint in Global Capitalism

The activist's discourse about TNCs, plant closing
legislation and capital mobility has been character-
istically indignant. When activists learn that a
conglomerate has closed a plant in an older area
even as it builds one abroad, the fact that this
shift is profitable to the firm seems to indict it.
The implication is that highest rates of return are
somehow a matter of choice, and the TNCs could, if
they willed it, settle for less. Nothing in the
history of capitalism suggests that this perspective
is accurate. While arguing it publicly has the
modest virtue of casting the conglomerates as
villains, it has the grave fault of implying that
large scale capitalist enterprises can thrive in the
long run without seeking the highest rates of return
and lowest labour militance.

As an invention of investors and employers, as
with all such massive shifts in social scale, the
TNC was born of necessity. While the pressure
experienced by these firms was competition from
other rivals, the strategy of conglomeration and
internationalisation is directed towards forcing
labour and taxpayers to bear the burden of that
competition. Consider the strategic implication of
the takeover, in the early 1970s of the largest
American producer of bread and baked goods –
Continental Baking – by ITT. Previous to Continental's acquisition, the union representing its workers
represented all of Continental production workers.
Once acquired, Continental's contribution to ITT's
overall corporate profits amounted to one percent.
The Bakery and Confectionery Workers Union was thus
shifted from a situation in which it could shut down
the employer to one in which it could jeopardise but
one percent of the employer's profits. This is a
change in power at the point of production, which is
paralleled by changes in relations of local political
power. As the TNC deploy their capital worldwide,
any national group of workers undergoes a similar
erosion in power. North American workers employed by
Ford, for example, work for an organisation which
gains most of its profits from foreign operations.

On the left, especially in the Western Hemi-
sphere, the analysis of advanced capitalism has
tended to focus on monopoly capitalism. Competition
among capitalists recedes in such perspectives, for
analysts generally focus on the market power and
price-making activity of the very large firms. Since
approximately the mid-1960s, however, competition
has affected investment behaviour with renewed

force. The encroachment of Japanese and European TNCs on traditional U.S. markets has forced U.S. firms to seek sites of production which provide cheap labour and strategies of industrial organisation which weaken domestic labour. Thus, in the commodity markets for television, radios, clothing, steel and autos, substantial proportions of U.S. domestic consumption is imported, even while substantial fractions of those imports may be controlled by U.S. capital. The growing control of TNCs over the world-wide resource allocation process is, therefore, a response to clear exigencies, and not caused by deficient sensibility.

These exigencies of global capitalism are the crucible of contemporary political strategies. On one hand, capitalists in industries threatened by foreign capital are leading, or attempting to lead, corporate-labour coalitions for protectionist trade policy. This accompanies a chauvinist ideological mobilisation using such pretexts as Soviet military force and the intervention in Afghanistan, as well as the hostage-taking in Iran. The atmosphere engendered encourages national cross-class solidarity, as distinct from international class solidarity. It asks workers to subsidise, in yet another form, corporate profits.

Alternatively, as we have seen, labour and progressive citizens groups have begun to develop policies at state and national levels to restrict the mobility of capital. The struggle for this legislation promises to unite workers in both their neighbourhood/citizen/consumer roles and their roles in production. But even if successful the strategy might not forestall change, for the costs incurred in such schemes would not be high enough to outweigh market considerations. Once one ventures beyond the moral critique of corporate behaviour, one must confront the probability that national regulation of capital allocation in the global context may simply be ineffective in maintaining or enhancing the position of the working class vis-a-vis capital.

This conclusion bears on two aspects of current political developments in North America. On the one hand, the populist movement rests on a pragmatic orientation toward the defence of working people's interest in local politics. It avoids characterising itself as socialist, but fosters both anti-corporate consciousness and a programmatic demand for more regulation. (We have seen, however, that local regulatory demands can be evaded and are subject to concerted attack by business activists.) On the other hand, through the Democratic Socialist Organizing Committee, and the Democratic Agenda within the Democratic Party, social democratic perspectives on economic planning and the social control of capital are gaining some ground among activists and intellectuals, and a small number of elected officials.

In this situation, the more vigorous, mass-based populists are unable to address the question of the social ownership of the means of production, while the more elite-based democratic socialist alternative is more or less committed to pursuing its political and strategic programme within the Democratic Party arena. The prospect of achieving a programme oriented to overcoming the power of the TNCs, and to sustaining levels of living in North America, through the party of Jimmy Carter, is not favourable. Thus, despite the renewal of genuinely working class dissent from national policy, there is no near-term prospect of a powerful political force which can, in very practical ways, project a programme of socially based solutions to capital allocation. Yet, the strategic dilemma is even more complex.

In 1976, many American observers were struck by the fact that the successful candidate for the Presidency had been introduced to major corporate and diplomatic circles through his participation in the Trilateral Commission. Formed through the initiative of David Rockefeller, the Trilateral Commission represents the recognition by financial and corporate capital in the advanced countries that co-ordination of state policies is necessary for an orderly transition to global capitalism. That President Carter chose important members of his Cabinet and staff from the Commission testified to the influence of such perspectives.

By contrast, American workers, and, we suspect, their European counterparts, formulate strategy and tactics very much within the confines of a national political perspective. There are exceptions in detail, we realise, but the fundamental strategic outlook of trade union, socialist and communist movements tends to presume that each national arena offers each working class the opportunity to improve its objective conditions, and even to transform social relations.

A recent American newspaper article on the troubles of the automobile industry suggests the inadequacy of such strategic views. Discussing nationalisation of the American auto industry in a speculative fashion, the article pointed out that very large proportions of the assets of the Big Three auto makers were held overseas. What would be the disposal of these assets in the event of nationalisation in the U.S., but no corresponding initiative in Europe or South America? Clearly, without the co-operation of other states, and other national communities of workers, such a tactic would fail.

In any case, the new world order of capitalism has changed the scale of class conflict, and thus the scale of appropriate progressive responses. Often, we become aware of great changes, we gain knowledge of large systems, only as they pass into history. In the older industrial regions of the U.S., the United Kingdom, France, and elsewhere, the social impacts of global capitalism were experienced far before workers and their allies understood it as a system. "The owl of Minerva", Hegel wrote, "takes flight at dusk".

REFERENCES

1. James R. O'Connor, The Fiscal Crisis of the State, New York: St. Martin's Press, 1973. In adopting O'Connor's fruitful concepts and terminology, we do not necessarily subscribe to the rest of his analysis.

2. William Kornblum, Blue Collar Community, Chicago: University of Chicago Press, 1974.

3. Barry Bluestone and Bennett Harrison, Capital and Communities, Washington, DC: Progressive Alliance, 1980.

4. Harvey Molotch, "The City As A Growth Machine", American Journal of Sociology, 82 (2), 1976, pp. 309-332.

5. Robert Ross, Don M. Shakow, and Paul Susman, "Local Planners - Global Constraints", Policy Sciences, 12 (1980), pp. 1-25.

6. International Union, United Automobile, Aerospace, and Agricultural Implement Workers of America (UAW), "A UAW Program to Get America Back to Work", Solidarity, Vol. 23, No. 5, May 1-15, 1980, pp. 12-13.

7. Joint Report of Labor Union Study Tour Participants, Economic Dislocation: Plant Closings, Plant Relocations, and Plant Conversion, May 1, 1978, Washington, DC, German Marshall Fund.

8. Manuel Castells, The Urban Question, Cambridge: MIT Press, 1977.

9. Kornblum, op. cit.

POLITICAL STATEMENT

Why should socialists be interested in understanding the unequal use which capital makes of space as it continuously restructures space?

Capital's production of space is basic to its aggressive strategy vis-a-vis the working class. Socialist analysis of regional change seeks to illuminate the nature of local changes within a framework which comprehends the overall spatial organisation of capitalism. Such spatial organisation reflects the structural dynamics of capital, the need for expanded reproduction. The knowledge generated can help support the struggle of the working class and the socialist movement with strategic insight and tactical information.

Let us specify this further:

A. Socialist analysis of regional or local events and trends attempts to overcome the current 'common sense' of bourgeois ideology. This ideology focuses on the character of the people in a place, or the geographic advantages or disadvantages of a given place from the point of view of capitalist class investors and functionaries. It portrays restructuring, especially decline, which negatively effects workers as 'natural' forces to which prudent citizens will acquiesce. By contrast, socialist discussion of regional problems intervenes in this 'normal' state of ideological confusion in a way which allows workers and their associations to recognise themselves as agents of historical process, and the capitalist class as their adversary. Thus, socialist analysis of regional change transcends the local context, identifying the powerful ways in which capitalism uses the uneven development of different places, the uneven production of the built environment, as a weapon in class conflict.

As a contribution to workers engaged in that struggle, socialist analysis attempts to produce the recognition, by each potential agent, of the place he or she occupies in the dominant system of capitalist relations of production: it aims to produce a class consciousness as a response to experience which presents itself to workers as <u>regional</u> phenomena. A socialist analysis of the 'regional problem' must produce a counter-ideology to that generated and reified by bourgeois regional analysis.

B. Socialist analysis of regions is an instrument of political calculation to be used by the working class. It must provide specific knowledge of the objective conditions which form the context of class positions. For example, regional analysis should clarify the bourgeois interest as a class agent in reproducing certain capitalist class relations manifest in particular spatial structures. This capital restructuring of the objective conditions of production and reproduction must be understood so that working class organisation and strategy can successfully react to its current threats. A socialist regional analysis must produce information about the system at present and develop adequate concepts with which to make effective class analysis.

C. Socialist analysis of regions has a strategic dimension. The socialist movement must respond to capital's creation and use of spatial differences with strategies of its own.

Intellectuals who respond to the socialist movement's needs make both a critical and a positive contribution to the movement's choice of strategic responses. In a given regional or national context, the movement may adopt strategies which appear appropriate to local experiences and traditions. Such strategies may appear more problematic when a more comprehensive view of many regional situations is considered. Socialists concerned with the 'regional problem' may participate in such discussion as will permit more adequate strategy to evolve. This activity generates guidelines by which the effectiveness of various strategies may be evaluated.

Socialist analysis of regional change is particularly concerned with the political dimension of worker's strategic responses. At whatever level, the economic, political or ideological, socialist contribution to strategy aims to discover demands that unite workers as a class, wherever they are. Such strategy aims to increase the power of the

working class, pointing towards the transformation
and overthrow of capitalist social relations.

A concern with these issues is expressed in the
work of all members of this group. In particular, we
have come to agreement on a number of crucial questions which relate to this political conception:

1. With regard to bourgeois ideology and its
implications for 'class consciousness':

So-called 'regional problems' in capitalist
society are actually the social and economic
problems which arise when an historically determined
spatial structure of this society is altered during
the process of capital accumulation as a consequence
of changing demands of individual capitals for their
conditions of production and reproduction. The ongoing imperative for the spatial structure of capitalist society to restructure reinforces spatial
inequality. This process and its manifestation as
the 'regional problem' is a political question for
the working class.

2. With regard to our analysis of the present
objective conditions facing the working class:

The working class is facing a situation which
presents specific difficulties for traditional
methods of labour's struggle.

(a) <u>International Reserve Army</u>
There is a new readiness on the part of capital
to migrate from regions of organised working
class activity to regions which have experienced little industrial development hitherto.
These regions offer special advantages in the
form of low-wage labour, high productivity,
political constraints on labour organising, and
so forth. This implies the creation of an
<u>international reserve army</u> serving to weaken
<u>the position of labour</u> vis-a-vis capital.

(b) <u>Internationalisation of Capital</u>
At the same time, capitalism has perfected
mechanisms of international capital transfer,
e.g. through the creation of transnational
firms.

(c) <u>Regional Problem</u>
The phenomena of heightened global capital
movement has created a critical problem for
mature industrial regions, especially those
experiencing capital outflow. These regions
constitute a major locus of struggle between
capital and labour in the present conjuncture -
implying that the issue of regional development, the regional problem, has a particular

degree of political importance at the present
time.
(d) The Importance of the Labour Process
While not uniform among sectors, there are
certain common tendencies in the labour process
which confer a strategic advantage to capital
in its struggle with labour.
- in some sectors, a differentiation over
space by function leading to a new spatial
division of labour
- a reduction in time required to mobilise
new elements into the labour force.
(e) The New Form of Imperialism
There have been significant changes in peripheral regions, particularly in the Third
World, as traditional patterns of imperialism
are modified through the growth of export
platforms and free trade zones.

3.   With regard to our political action and its
relationship to socialist transformation:
At this present conjuncture, in order to continue to challenge 'common sense' or bourgeois
ideology, we are compelled to analyse the structural
constraints upon successful working class action by
broadening the scope of our regional analyses to
incorporate the international dimension. International collaborative research enables us to more
adequately apprehend the present objective conditions of working class struggle. Such research
focusing on the interconnections between regional
problems can provide knowledge of the system and of
the way struggles are being waged in our respective
locations.
The results of our analyses can then be used by
agents of struggle in a variety of places, informing
local struggles with a vision of their international
dimension.